Praise for
Innovation the Cleveland Clinic Way

"While progress in research and technology hold tremendous potential to improve human health, the healthcare industry must also contend with unprecedented change and complex challenges. Tom Graham offers far-sighted and practical strategies for applying technology to democratize and accelerate health innovation. Approaches like these are exactly what is needed to transform healthcare and realize its potential to help us lead healthier and more productive lives."

—MIKE RHODIN, Senior Vice President,
IBM Watson and Watson Health

"Innovation the Cleveland Clinic Way is a jewel of a book. Brilliantly written and phenomenally insightful, it explains in lucid terms the philosophy, framework, approach, and operation of a successful innovation engine in a large mission-driven organization. It combines theory and practice—as all good how-to books should—for building a real innovation juggernaut. Breathtaking in both scope and story, Tom Graham weaves insights from his own personal brush with death from medical illness together with the wisdom and experience he has garnered as the leader of the single most successful innovation enterprise sited within a healthcare system. It is a must-read."

—MARK SMITH, MD, Chief Innovation Officer,
MedStar Health and Director,
MedStar Institute for Innovation

"The industry is ripe for disruption. Dr. Graham brilliantly crystallizes the lessons learned and approaches honed at Cleveland Clinic, which can be leveraged by innovators to translate ideas into improved healthcare for all."

—DANIEL KRAFT, MD, Chair for Medicine,
Singularity University and Founder
and Chair, Exponential Medicine

"What else would you do with a master surgeon who is also a prolific inventor and serial entrepreneur but make him the Chief Innovation Officer of one of the most progressive institutions in all of healthcare? Tom Graham and Cleveland Clinic have truly written the book on how to build and sustain the architecture for innovation."

—NEIL JORDAN, Worldwide General Manager,
Healthcare Industry,
Microsoft Corporation

"Through Tom Graham's leadership, Cleveland Clinic is unlocking the potential for medical innovation and commercialization by building an ecosystem to compete with the best around the world. His collaborative approach that brings together academia, companies, and other institutional players is part of an effective innovation strategy that is driving talent attraction, job creation, and large-scale economic development."

—JOHN MINOR, CEO, JobsOhio

"Healthcare is in the midst of a remarkable metamorphosis and while this disruption is uncomfortable for many influencers in the industry, Dr. Graham embraces it and is forging the road ahead. A gifted surgeon, respected innovator, consummate collaborator—and survivor—Dr. Graham brings a unique perspective to the next era of healthcare, and is an inspirational catalyst for both its defragmentation and transformation in the digital age."

—JEFF ARNOLD, Founder, WebMD,
and CEO, Sharecare

"Medical innovation is severely challenged by risks and realities like the capital gap, the patent cliff, and Eroom's Law. Cleveland Clinic has managed to buck the trend by focusing on process and collaboration. Their Chief Innovation Officer is talking—everyone in the innovation ecosystem should listen."

—ANDREW LO, PhD, CHARLES E. and SUSAN T. HARRIS
Professor of Finance and Director of the
Laboratory for Financial Engineering,
MIT Sloan School of Management

"Dr. Graham is a renowned expert on innovation and a prolific inventor in his own right. Working closely with him and Cleveland Clinic for years has proven invaluable for our organization, particularly in the evaluation and commercialization process. Simply put, innovation is in the DNA and culture of Cleveland Clinic. Yet cultures of innovation require inspired leadership, and with Dr. Thomas Graham and Dr. Toby Cosgrove, Cleveland Clinic has forged a place at the forefront of the world of healthcare innovation."

—JOE RANDOLPH, President and CEO,
The Innovation Institute

"Big ideas, when put to work, change the world. In this book, Dr. Tom Graham inspires us with his successful strategy and galvanizing vision. Academic, corporate, philanthropic, and public policy goals can all be achieved when we invest in innovation. Humanity wins in this ultimate team sport."

—AARON PITTS, Managing Director,
JobsOhio

Innovation
the
Cleveland Clinic Way

Innovation
the
Cleveland Clinic Way

Powering Transformation
by Putting Ideas to Work

Thomas J. Graham, MD
Chief Innovation Officer of Cleveland Clinic

New York Chicago San Francisco Athens London Madrid
Mexico City Milan New Delhi Singapore Sydney Toronto

1 2 3 4 5 6 7 8 9 0   QFR/QFR   1 2 1 0 9 8 7 6 5

ISBN   978-1-259-58295-0
MHID   1-259-58295-7

e-ISBN   978-1-259-58296-7
e-MHID   1-259-58296-5

This publication is designed to provide accurate and authoritative information
in regard to the subject matter covered. It is sold with the understanding that
neither the author nor the publisher is engaged in rendering legal, accounting,
securities trading, or other professional services. If legal advice or other expert
assistance is required, the services of a competent professional person should
be sought.
   —*From a Declaration of Principles Jointly Adopted by a Committee of the
      American Bar Association and a Committee of Publishers and Associations*

Library of Congress Cataloging-in-Publication Data

Graham, Thomas J.
Innovation the Cleveland Clinic way : powering transformation by putting
   ideas to work / by Thomas J Graham, MD.
New York : McGraw-Hill, [2016]
LCCN 2015040576| ISBN 9781259582950 (hardback) | ISBN 1259582957
   (hardback)
Medical care—Technological innovations. | Medical technology. |
   BISAC: BUSINESS & ECONOMICS / Entrepreneurship.
LCC R855.3 .G73 2016 | DDC 610.285—dc23 LC record available at
   http://lccn.loc.gov/2015040576

To my family—CeCe, Margaret, and Libby. Thanks for a lifetime of joy and sticking by me when it looked like all was lost.

To my friends—especially Mark, Bill, Jim, Sean, Joe, Tim, Frank, Tom, and Jack. I was never blessed with siblings, but that didn't mean I was without brothers.

To my colleagues—Toby, Joe, Brian, and all my partners at Cleveland Clinic. I've stood on the shoulders of many giants; I hope to make you proud.

To my caregivers—Matt, Sri, Mark, Chuck, and all the others, giving me more time with your skill and caring is my life's greatest gift.

To my patients—I thank every one of you for your sacred trust.

Contents

Preface

Anil Jain came to Cleveland Clinic right out of medical school in 1998, just as we were pioneering a new approach to medical record keeping—the electronic medical record or EMR, which eliminated cumbersome paper files, reduced medical errors, and allowed doctors to enter and retrieve patient data at the touch of a keyboard.

A dedicated physician, Dr. Jain is also a self-described health information technology (HIT) "nut." He perceived that the EMR could be a fount of knowledge for medical researchers, with its millions of patient data points, trackable across time and robust with information on the inception, progress, and treatment of every possible disease condition.

But the information was locked behind firewalls, buried in incompatible systems, and protected by laws ensuring patient privacy. Dr. Jain knew what was needed—a tool to liberate the data in the EMR and make it available to the research community. He took time from his patient care schedule to work on the problem. Through trial and error, he developed a search engine, which he called e-Research. This Google-like application allowed researchers to scour hundreds of thousands of patient records and pinpoint relevant data sets in seconds.

What made Dr. Jain's search engine particularly valuable was that he'd found a way to strip the records of all patient names and other identifying characteristics. This cloaking feature would make it possible for other hospitals and medical centers to open up their EMRs without fear of compromising patient security, exponentially increasing the value to researchers.

Dr. Jain had invented an exciting new HIT product that could aid researchers, help patients, generate income for Cleveland Clinic, and potentially emerge as a new company boosting the regional economy.

How did he move this valuable and tested idea to the marketplace? How did it get a patent? How did it raise capital and attract partners? Dr. Jain found the assistance he needed right at Cleveland Clinic Innovations (CCI), our experienced, well-organized, and mission-driven in-house technology development, commercialization, and corporate venturing unit. Since 2004, CCI has executed some 600 licenses for innovations and spun off 70-plus companies, attracting nearly a billion dollars in investment capital.

CCI introduced Dr. Jain to two experienced digital entrepreneurs who were looking for a new challenge in the health sphere. They licensed his application and scaled it up around a new architecture that could handle even more data from more sources. They called their company Explorys. CCI provided office space as well as legal, accounting, and marketing assistance for a stake in the emerging enterprise.

Today, Explorys is an enormous version of Dr. Jain's original search engine. Its massive server farms hold a clinical data set of more than 50 million lives. The company grew from 2 to 150 employees. The tool is now used by more than two dozen healthcare systems and nearly 400 hospitals to identify patterns in disease incidence, treatment, and outcome.

In 2015, Explorys was acquired by IBM to be integrated into IBM Watson Health, a global big data project whose objective is to transform medicine, medical education, and medical spending for the twenty-first century. It's an illustration of Cleveland Clinic innovation at its best—putting ideas to work.

Since its founding in 1921, Cleveland Clinic has contributed some of the most important techniques and technologies advancing medical science. So it's not surprising that we've also pioneered the modern approach to innovation. Cleveland Clinic was at the vanguard among academic institutions who embraced the commercialization of intellectual property (IP). We leveraged our intellectual capacity for discovery and honed methodologies for technology development. The result was that Cleveland Clinic best processes for technology transfer have become best practices in medical innovation that now reach beyond just healthcare and its adjacent sectors to guide the practice innovation across all domains.

As chief innovation officer of Cleveland Clinic, I've had a front-row seat and a modest hand in developing one of the world's foremost innovation engines and am inspired to open the door to its home base each day. I've tasted both the fruits and disappointments that accompany innovation, while also being the beneficiary of its magic to heal. I've touched or been touched by almost every facet of innovation. I've benefited from my pursuit of creative ideas and wish to share how to derive success and significance from solving problems.

This book was expressly designed for the engaged practitioner of innovation—or those who aspire to achieve expertise and leadership in its practice. Innovation occurs best at the intersection of knowledge domains and is catalyzed by collaboration. Reducing transcendent ideas to practice takes disciplined processes and is a metrics-driven pursuit. I seek to share the key ingredients and enablers that have distinguished CCI. Some terms, ideas, concepts, theories, organizations, and institutions may not be discussed at great length at first mention, but in these cases, brief introductory definitions and descriptions will be provided.

I'm transparent about the challenges along the way and also emphasize the importance of teamwork. Innovation is not a linear journey, and neither is developing a sustainable engine to capture it. Making innovation a sustainable priority on the individual and institutional level is just as much about the *why* as the *how*. If the fundamental reasons an individual or organization innovates are aligned with mission, even the most complex organization can operate its innovation engine efficiently and successfully.

This is not just a book; it's simultaneously a passport and an invitation. It's your passport to Cleveland Clinic's journey to primacy in pursuit of innovation excellence. It contains the practical instruments we use every day and the mechanisms to reach out to us for assistance.

This is also an invitation to join a movement. Whether or not you're involved in healthcare, you can become a practitioner of mission-driven innovation. The journey begins with the motivation behind why you're in business, then embraces disciplined processes that gestate creative ideas to the marketplace. This is meant to be an inspiring playbook for assessing and executing the operational and cultural elements that define the successful high-innovation organization.

The Cleveland Clinic way is to be the best partner in modern healthcare. It starts with our own patients and caregivers and extends to our professional and residential communities and the world beyond.

There's no higher calling than improving and extending human life. This is the story of the individuals and institution that pioneered mission-driven innovation and achieved a balance between doing good and doing well. Adopt these principles, identify your industry's higher calling, and join the creative community that puts ideas to work. Accept the innovation challenge!

Acknowledgments

The practice of innovation, like that of medicine, is a team sport. Through the course of writing this book, I learned that authorship is also a collective pursuit.

The roster of mentors, colleagues, friends, and inspirations is long, and I fear that I may inadvertently fail to include all in these acknowledgments. I could have simply recognized my Cleveland Clinic colleagues as a group because we're an organization that lives by our motto "To act as a unit"—and I have benefited from this as a member of that community and as a patient—nevertheless, I want to recognize some of the valued contributors who made this book possible.

Cleveland Clinic CEO and president Toby Cosgrove deserves the pole position in this section for a multitude of reasons. His vision for and leadership of our organization has transformed Cleveland Clinic from a regionally dominant healthcare system to an international medical resource. His personal history as an inventor and his dedication to making innovation a cornerstone of our institutional identity enables CCI to flourish. I am humbled that he named me Cleveland Clinic's inaugural chief innovation officer. Through the *Cleveland Clinic Way* series, he empowered our organization to share its experiences and expertise to help transform all of healthcare.

In the early 1990s, Joe Hahn was my mentor in developing the concepts that eventually led to CCI, while simultaneously guiding my career in his role as Cleveland Clinic's chief of surgery. In my decade away from Cleveland Clinic, Joe, as the physician-leader and steward of CCI, built the infrastructure on which it stands today. One of the major reasons I returned to Cleveland was to work again with Joe in his capacity as chief of staff. There is no person I have known of greater integrity and humanism. As a physician, executive, family man, and human being, there is no better role model.

Also preceding me in authorship of a book in the *Cleveland Clinic Way* series is my friend Jim Merlino. As former chief experience officer of Cleveland Clinic, he pioneered many of the programs that solidified Cleveland Clinic as a leader in engagement and empathetic treatment. His *Service Fanatics* is a great read that captures the essence of our organization's "Patients First" philosophy.

Linda McHugh is executive administrator to the CEO and Board of Governors. She is not only a key contributor to the success of our organization, but also an advocate for telling our story through vehicles such as the *Cleveland Clinic Way* series. She is a prime mover behind the scenes. Her enthusiasm for what we do at Cleveland Clinic is equaled only by her loyalty to the institution and its mission.

Six other Cleveland Clinic officers or trustees have been exceptionally influential in my professional journey to becoming the chief innovation officer: The late Fred Loop was the CEO when we first executed on partnering the individual with the institution for the IP estate in its contemporary model. Bob Rich, CEO of Rich Products Corporation, was the chairman of the Board of Trustees who planted the seed for me to return to Cleveland after a decade in Baltimore. Joe Scaminace, the board vice chairman, has been a treasured friend and business advisor, while setting an example as the successful CEO of OM Group. Tom Wamberg, a gifted thinker and successful innovator, has been a close confidant and has interjected entrepreneurial spirit and philanthropy into CCI. Pat Auletta has brought his deep knowledge in sophisticated finance to tutor me on how to perpetuate our function through times of plenty and austerity. Finally, Harry Rein has made untold contributions to CCI in his many roles as chairman of our various advisory bodies and as a staunch advocate for innovation in the academic setting.

I've published extensively in hand surgery—I didn't know how easy I had it writing about a subject where the basics of anatomy and biomechanics don't change. When you are writing about a complex, dynamic topic like innovation, it's a real challenge. I was blessed to have the expert assistance of four fantastic editors. Beth Brumbaugh is a skilled and experienced collaborator whom I luckily "inherited" from Jim Merlino. I know how much my writing improved during our exchanges; her deft touch allowed me to tell my story and that of CCI in my own words while making it more accessible to you.

There is probably no individual more fluent in both the English language and the culture of Cleveland Clinic than Steve Szilagyi. He guided my thoughts and words in a way that brings the topic and the organization to life. Editorial assistance from Cleveland Clinic's Bob Smith was valuable in guiding the book over the finish line. He showed skill and passion for the project, which positively influenced its outcome.

I have learned a great deal from McGraw-Hill publications over the years and am humbled now to be on the other side of the page as an author. The high quality of McGraw-Hill's books is due in large part to editors such as Casey Ebro, with whom I had the pleasure to work. She had an amazing vision for this book and the entire series. It is a special gift to be a great storyteller, but to do it by guiding the pen of several authors is truly exceptional. I thank her for her support and guidance.

My quarter-century as a physician and my 14 months as a patient uniquely qualify me as a veteran provider and consumer. In the book, I say that "innovation saved my life"—more correctly, innovation in the hands of engaged and expert caregivers saved my life. There's practically nobody at Cleveland Clinic who didn't participate in my care, but four individuals really steered the ship: Drs. Matt Walsh, Sri Chalikonda, Mark Baker, and Chuck O'Malley. The fact is that I simply would not be here without them and the countless nurses, therapists, techs, housekeeping staff, food service employees, valets, and others who make up the Cleveland Clinic family.

As a servant leader, I truly work with and for a great group of professionals at CCI. I hope you'll visit our website (www.clevelandclinic.org/innovations) to learn more about our function and our team, each of whom brings unique perspectives and skills to grow and sustain our primacy. I am unable to list them all by name here, but I do want to recognize one former and one contemporary leader. Chris Coburn was a critical pioneer and partner in bringing CCI to its leadership position. Brian Kolonick leads our Global Healthcare Innovations Alliance with deep enthusiasm and intelligence.

The efforts of CCI have been buoyed by the sagacious advice of so many Innovation Advisory Board (IAB) members over the years who deserve a great deal of credit for our success. Dennis Kass, who has enjoyed a spectacular career on Wall Street and in public service, introduced me to Andrew Lo, one of the world's foremost economists, who has become my close friend and advisor over matters that will help perpetuate the mission-driven innovation ecosystem. I particularly want to recognize Steve Lindseth, Brad Vale, and Joe Cunningham, who have always extended their personal experience as entrepreneurs to me.

The professional staff that keeps me going every day, while juggling my clinical and executive duties, deserves equal credit: Michele Koballa, executive secretary; David Racela, nurse; and Nancy Sanders, clinical secretary, perform an amazing balancing act daily with aplomb and grace.

Innovators and patients are the reasons CCI exists; they're why Cleveland Clinic exists. CCI serves our abundant creative population, a community of innovators that is unparalleled. Underlying all I have done as a doctor, executive, or inventor is the dedication to improve and extend human life. There is no greater calling than to assist your fellow human beings, especially in their time of need. Whether you do this in a scrub suit or business suit, it is a noble aspiration and the prime motivator for our work and this book.

Preparation

"The future belongs to those who seize the opportunities created by innovation."

—TOBY COSGROVE, CEO and president
of Cleveland Clinic

Innovation's Logical Laboratory

Innovation invokes disciplined practice and results-oriented objectives that can distinguish an institution and deliver a sustainable competitive advantage. At Cleveland Clinic, innovation means putting ideas to work.

There may be no industry more in need of innovative thinking right now than healthcare. Everyone has gotten the memo. A fundamental paradigm shift in business models and relationship structures is demanded. No stakeholder is immune. Whether you're a provider, consumer, supplier, academic, elected official, or just an observer, you need to strap on your helmet.

What you do after buckling the chin strap will likely determine how your organization emerges from the turmoil. Some will bury their heads in the sand, the ostrich mentality. And there will be plenty of cut-to-prosperity advocates and stay-the-course proponents. But these pages are dedicated to those who intend to *innovate to improvement*—improvement in quality and outcomes, patient access, and increased fiscal responsibility.

This book is for those who've donned a crash helmet *and* a thinking cap, because you'll need both to survive and thrive. To think and execute the way out of this—and subsequent—quagmires will require innovation mastery.

Innovation is hard, elusive to achieve, and challenging to sustain. Shortcomings result from misunderstanding the merits of failure, inadequate engagement in disciplined innovation practices, and too little definition regarding why your institution innovates in the first place.

From the very inception of Cleveland Clinic, engaging in innovation wasn't just a novelty or opportunity, it was a responsibility. Innovation is a practice expressed in the very DNA of Cleveland Clinic. Innovation aligned with, amplified, and enabled our core belief that we're here to improve and extend human life.

We're often asked, "When did innovation begin at Cleveland Clinic?" The answer is easy: 1921. That's the year Cleveland Clinic was founded by four visionary physicians who'd served in U.S. Army hospitals during World War I and came home deeply impressed by the collaborative nature of military medicine. Our founders envisioned specialists with advanced knowledge and skill being deployed to focus on patients with complex problems. This model contradicted the jack-of-all-trades approach that abounded in medicine at the turn of the twentieth century.[1] Today, more physicians are engaged in professional arrangements such as Cleveland Clinic's than in traditional private practice.[2]

We're also often asked how Cleveland Clinic became so accomplished at innovation. Our group practice model is one of the principle catalysts. Our institution is full of clinical entrepreneurs who identify unmet needs, think creatively, share data, and ultimately provide solutions that advance the art and science of medicine. But we're also the highest-acuity hospital in the nation,[3] meaning we have the sickest patients. Our hands and brains became very adept at solving difficult problems.

Structurally and operationally, Cleveland Clinic became an innovation laboratory. Consider some of the medical breakthroughs that have been the result:

- Invention of the condenser dosimeter to measure therapeutic radiation (1928)

- The isolation and naming of serotonin and synthesis of angiotensin, key factors in hypertension (1940s–1950s)

- Development of renovascular surgery for hypertension (1950s)

- The first identification of carpal tunnel syndrome and the development of a diagnostic test for the condition (1951)

- Improvement of the kidney dialysis machine and first hospital-based dialysis unit (1950s)

- Invention of a unique heart-lung machine and its use in pioneering "stopped heart" surgery (1956)

- The discovery of coronary angiography, launching the modern age of interventional cardiology and cardiovascular surgery (1958)

- Invention of the intra-aortic balloon pump for temporary circulatory support (1962)

- Proving the viability of cadaver kidney transplants (1963)

- The first published coronary artery bypass surgery (1967)

- The discovery of a brain-mapping technique to locate the site of epileptic seizures (1980s)

- The first successful larynx transplant (1998)

- The first molecular test for thyroid cancer (2008)

- The first near-total face transplant (2008)

- Advanced endovascular stent graft design allowing expanded use of minimally invasive alternatives to surgery for aortic aneurysms (2009)

- Discovery of a microflora link to cardiovascular disease and development of a laboratory assay for risk (2011)

- Development of apps to provide portable and objective assessment of concussion and multiple sclerosis (2013)

- Creation of a web-based tool to assess individual risk for heritable and genetic disease (2013)

Cleveland Clinic founder George Washington Crile was an innovator on a grand scale. In addition to being the architect for the pioneering model of care for Cleveland Clinic, he also introduced advances as a master surgeon. Tools such as the carotid clamp, needle holder, and Crile forceps remain in use today. He is one of history's most recognized endocrine surgeons, perfecting procedures for goiter and other thyroid afflictions. In addition, Dr. Crile developed cannulas to conduct blood transfusion and was the first to utilize them successfully in the surgical theater and perform "human to human" transfusion. This gave him a technique to combat shock, to which he dedicated a great deal of his scholarly endeavor. His son, George "Barney" Crile Jr., was a famous physician-innovator in his own right, advocating less invasive surgeries for mastectomy, appendectomy, and drainage of pilonidal cysts and opposing unnecessary surgery, which was controversial at the time but is now widely lauded.

The Criles set an example for all Cleveland Clinic physicians to follow. For instance, modern cardiac care arose at Cleveland Clinic in the decade between F. Mason Sones's discovery of coronary angiography in 1958 and cardiac surgeon René Favaloro's pioneering coronary artery bypass grafting in 1967. Willem Kolff's work on the artificial kidney in the 1950s, the success of Ralph Straffon and Bruce Hubbard Stewart with cadaver kidney transplant in the 1960s, and Maria Siemionow and her team's performance of the first near-total face transplant in 2008 are among the achievements that have established Cleveland Clinic's reputation as one of the world's most robust clinical innovators.

Vanguard of Mission-Driven Innovation

Whether the invention has its genesis at the laboratory bench or patient bedside, the motivation behind innovation can prove to be the factor critical to success. *Mission-driven innovation* may sound fundamentally incongruous. Can organizations respond to growing performance pressures and care delivery expectations by pursuing commercialization of their intellectual property (IP) without corrupting their fundamentals? The philosophical underpinnings of academic medical centers (AMCs) and research universities provide motivation, direction, and necessary cohesiveness to some of the most potent creativity in our country. We staunchly maintain that *mission is the catalyst, not the barrier, to innovation.* Any organization can leverage the power of innovation to go on offense, while being true to its values.

Healthcare is not an industry that can allow others to solve its problems—our ingrained beliefs around the sanctity of human life, patient safety, and community service inform every decision we make. That's why we must leverage a special brand of innovation to tackle issues critical to our own organizations and the entire system.

As an orthopaedic surgeon and inventor for nearly three decades, *innovation* once meant coming up with a new device that addressed a specific problem or "fixed" a flaw. Today, the problems innovation seeks to solve seem far more broad and sophisticated. We grapple with acquiring and retaining patients by providing not only superior clinical outcomes but an exceptional patient experience. We strive to optimize point-of-care diagnostic testing, especially for chronic diseases, to support more patient-centered approaches to healthcare delivery. We wrestle with the role of technology as enabler in delivering better access and outcomes, especially in the handling of big data sets.

We continue to innovate on new devices and drugs; those remain part of the solution to improving care for patients and the population. We've simply widened the aperture regarding why we innovate and the mechanisms by which we innovate. The overwhelming good news is that the basic practice of innovation is the same, whether addressing improvement of an implant or improvement of an integrated system.

The fundamentals of identifying and resourcing creative minds remain constant. Removing barriers and accepting failure without penalizing the innovator remain relevant in healthcare and every business. Protecting innovation against the impact of wide swings in the market is the mark of commitment.

Mission-driven innovation doesn't disregard the fundamentals of the marketplace, but it follows a path illuminated by purpose. Cleveland Clinic embraced that concept from its origin and continues to practice it today. We've shown that you can *do well* and *do good* by staying firmly rooted in mission while demonstrating the adaptability needed to remain a leader in changing times.

Mission-driven innovation can be practiced by all. It is my hope to ignite mission-driven innovation in the individual and the institution alike and to encourage collaboration among practitioners.

Innovations at Cleveland Clinic: Turning Innovation into a Discipline

Cleveland Clinic Innovations (CCI), the commercialization and corporate venturing arm of Cleveland Clinic, is charged with developing creative thought and translating it to the marketplace. Innovation has become one of Cleveland Clinic's core competencies and touches nearly all of our endeavors. We've woven disciplined creativity into the tapestry of our institutional culture and now teach other healthcare systems and commercial partners to do the same.

Cleveland Clinic formalized a process and built a sustainable infrastructure for developing and commercializing IP. In parallel to our clinical and scientific breakthroughs, we were innovating the way innovation itself was practiced.

1920s to 1960s

In Dr. Crile's day, it was not uncommon for surgeons to develop devices to be used for an individual patient. Doctors often used their home workshops to fabricate instruments that facilitated a particular test or treatment, and a professional toolmaker and glassblower were on staff. They were the *prototype* of today's prototype shop.

It's believed that the first Cleveland Clinic staff member to receive and market a patent was Maria Telkes, a pioneering biophysicist and inventor who had a distinguished academic and industrial career. In 1930, she applied for a patent for an "electro-osmotic generator," possibly for use in Dr. Crile's research on the conductivity of human tissue.

At least as early as 1931, director of biomedical research D. Roy McCullagh was licensing his inventions for commercialization and directing at least a portion of the proceeds back to Cleveland Clinic. A part of his interests was spun off to found Ben Venue Laboratories, Inc., which researched the manufacture of blood plasma and penicillin.

The period after World War II was an active one for clinical and scientific breakthroughs, but procedures such as coronary angiography and open-heart surgery were not protected from an IP standpoint.

1970s to 1990s

In 1970, a new department called Biomedical Engineering (later changed to Clinical Engineering) was launched to inspire physicians then pioneering the field of electronic medical equipment to concentrate development in-house and inspire commercialization.

This process started to accelerate in 1980 with passage of the University and Small Business Patent Procedures Act, known as the Bayh-Dole Act, authored by U.S. Senators Birch Bayh (D-IN) and Robert Dole (R-KS). Prior to the act, medical discoveries stemming from the billions in government-sponsored research were considered to be federal property; this was a disincentive for innovators and their institutions. Of the 30,000 patents sponsored by federal research accumulated before 1980, only 1,500 were ever licensed to companies, and researchers were never accorded a share of generated proceeds.[4]

The Bayh-Dole Act allowed innovations derived from AMCs and universities to move beyond research results consigned to scientific journals to healthcare products with the power to improve and extend human life. The act required that academic institutions share royalties resulting from the commercial development of taxpayer-supported inventions with those making the discovery.

Coupled with U.S. patent protection law and evolving technology-transfer capabilities on academy campuses, the Bayh-Dole Act has been a major driving force behind medical innovation and economic growth over the past three decades. Technology transfer is the assignment of technology IP from the originator to a secondary user through means such as licensing.

Cleveland Clinic was well positioned to take advantage of the new landscape and was among the first to recognize and embrace the act's power. In 1984, the Board of Governors initiated a study to determine the commercial feasibility of marketing Cleveland Clinic research efforts. An Office of New Enterprises was formed, with John H. Rogers as its first director.

The charter for the new entity was quite forward-looking—to develop commercially viable products derived from healthcare technologies and research and to identify business opportunities and maximize returns. This statement goes beyond the traditional definition of technology transfer to recognize that the power of innovation is derived from identifying business opportunities. A flurry of technology commercialization activity followed that allowed Cleveland Clinic to assume leadership in innovation.

Several years before my arrival, Toby Cosgrove, a world-renowned cardiac surgeon before becoming Cleveland Clinic CEO and president, had developed a closed-loop system for drug administration to improve arterial blood pressure following cardiac surgery. He found an outside patent attorney and some external engineers, and he convinced a company to manufacture his invention. Dr. Cosgrove never forgot the pride he felt handing over a check for a $50,000 donation from his royalty payments to then–chief executive William Kiser. Here was monetary proof that clinical innovation mattered. Dr. Cosgrove opened the door to technology transfer as a surrogate for translational research, the application of basic research findings to enhance human health. Our talented clinicians could be the source for IP that could be commercialized in ways in which both the inventor and the institution could benefit.

Dr. Cosgrove remains one of the most prolific inventors in Cleveland Clinic history, with his "Cosgrove ring" for mitral valve repair being among the most lucrative royalty-producing patents in the organization's portfolio. The fact that he has taken the journey as an inventor undoubtedly fuels his continued support of the innovation function and his vision of how it can be a difference-maker for an individual and an institution. More important, he understands and embraces that ultimately innovation serves patients.

It doesn't take a business degree to deduce that the longer individuals or institutions maintain control of their IP, the more valuable and remunerative it becomes to the originator. One of the hardest concepts to communicate to inventors remains protection of IP and how licensing and syndicated investing works. Logically, if you invent something, you should own it, but that is not always so. The disconnect between what our inventors believed to be true and the practices of the "real world" was permitting a great deal of IP to leak out of Cleveland Clinic and result in inferior deals for our creative staff.

Sensing that I was not the only staff member reluctant to let my ideas go over the transom directly to industry without participation, I approached then-CEO Floyd D. Loop about how we could use the formal process that was evolving under the Office of Technology Transfer to partner the institution and the individual and share the proceeds. Dr. Loop referred me to my supervisor and personal mentor, Dr. Joseph F. Hahn, an accomplished neurosurgeon and inventor who was chairman of the Division of Surgery.

As he has been throughout my career, Dr. Hahn was a great navigator. Two aspects were pioneering about our accessing Cleveland Clinic's emerging technology-transfer function: (1) Despite having so many clinical breakthroughs throughout our history, the technology-transfer apparatus was thought to be largely about commercializing scientific research; and (2) this effort was the first to rely on a completely internal process for development and a codified revenue sharing arrangement between the inventor and the institution.

We enlisted general counsel Michael J. Meehan to act as our original patent attorney to safeguard the IP. At that time, Cleveland Clinic maintained a small biomechanical engineering group under Dr. Cornhill's tutelage. The group modified surgical implants for research purposes and made some devices to employ in patient care, just like back in Dr. Crile's day. This became our original prototype lab.

We were able to take advantage of Cleveland Clinic's pioneering concept of uniting under one roof all the elements necessary to operate a full-scale technology-transfer and commercialization apparatus. Combining the intellectual, technical, legal, regulatory, and transactional components for the purpose of controlling and transacting on IP was a departure in the practice of innovation. Instead of simply being a set of "bookends," originating the ideas and then purchasing the finished products from industry to employ them on behalf of patients, Cleveland Clinic became a full-service innovation development engine.

As the millennium approached, we used my early patents to pilot the full-service or one-stop-shop concept of technology development and commercialization. We had negotiated a license with Biomet, Inc. for the first product on which Cleveland Clinic and I partnered, the BioSymMetRic™ External Fixator, a device used to treat complex fracture-dislocations of the knuckles. To this day, Cleveland Clinic and I receive royalties on its sales.

As 2000 approached, Cleveland Clinic became increasingly sophisticated regarding IP-related business opportunities and aware of how important it could be for recruitment, retention, and reward. From our more rudimentary technology-transfer beginnings, our contemporary innovation function was developing. We'd demonstrated that creative ideas weren't limited to the laboratory bench. We recognized that capital infusion at critical times could be just as influential on successful IP development as the quality of the idea itself. In 1997, Cleveland Clinic established NovaMedics, Inc., for the express purpose of creating spin-off companies and managing the venture investing functions of the enterprise.

By 1999, Cleveland Clinic had committed to its present-day commercialization model. To have in place the technical architecture, funding mechanisms, and industry relationships was of considerable appeal to all at Cleveland Clinic who wished to engage in the development of new solutions. We were enthusiastic to be part of a culture that embraced innovation and valued intellectual contributions.

2000 to the Present

In early 2000, Dr. Loop charged Dr. Hahn and Chris Coburn to develop and manage the commercialization arm of Cleveland Clinic. Chris had just been recruited from Battelle Institute. He had spent the previous year as a consultant evaluating the commercialization effort at Cleveland Clinic, which was still under the Office of Technology Transfer.

Together, Chris and Dr. Hahn built Cleveland Clinic Innovations from the ground up. The name covered all innovation efforts. CCI had virtually all the resources it needed: space for small spin-off companies, project incubators with labs, engineers to develop drawings and prototypes, patent attorneys, licensing experts, legal experts, government agency experts, and other inventors. This arrangement was the commercialization model to fulfill the mantra of "bench to bedside" in an efficient way.

Understanding the capital requirements of emerging technologies, Cleveland Clinic supported a venture capital fund in which it was a significant investor, Foundation Medical Partners. The fund operated at arm's length but benefited from the market insight and reputation of Cleveland Clinic. Now called Flare Capital Partners, it has raised subsequent funds and continues to work cooperatively with Cleveland Clinic.

The period since 2000 marked the exceptional growth of Cleveland Clinic as a leader in mission-driven innovation. We've invested millions of dollars and countless hours in developing a core competency in commercial development of IP. We've concentrated on process, developed proprietary instruments to evaluate ideas for clinical or scientific merit, and invited experienced advisory experts from industry and the investment sector to evaluate market feasibility.

In 2001, a major new event was launched, the Cleveland Clinic Medical Innovation Summit. Chris and Dr. Hahn started this as a national showcase for the latest developments in healthcare technology and delivery. It brought together clinical experts, inventors, government agencies (including the Centers for Medicare & Medicaid Services), venture investors, and marketing experts. CEOs from major companies presented their strategies and plans for the future of healthcare. The summit has become the Super Bowl of medical innovation, attracting nearly 2,000 colleagues to Cleveland each autumn.

After a 10-year period as director of the Curtis National Hand Center in Baltimore, I returned to Cleveland Clinic in 2010 to witness what decades of dedication to advancing creative thought can accomplish. The hard work and vision of so many talented individuals, amplified by their desire to assist humankind, had resulted in a robust operating platform already distinguishing itself as a pioneer in the field of mission-driven innovation. I had the privilege to work with Chris until his departure to assume innovation leadership responsibilities at Partners HealthCare in Boston.

Along with Cleveland Clinic trustee and key Innovation Advisory Board member Harry T. Rein, we sought to build on the foundation that was established in the first decade of CCI's existence by optimizing our organizational design and operational platform. CCI has learned to balance company creation with technology licensing to develop a billion-dollar portfolio of holdings. We've spun off more than 70 companies, managed some 600 royalty-bearing licenses, attracted almost $1 billion in equity investment and commercialization grants, and created over 1,500 jobs. And we've made what we've learned over the decades scalable and transferable to other organizations through our Global Healthcare Innovations Alliance.

This book tells you exactly how we've done it.

Philosophy

Where Should Innovation
Be Conducted and by Whom?

There's no one "correct" philosophy of innovation. Individuals, institutions, commercial entities, academic medical centers (AMCs), and research universities all have differing philosophies regarding commercialization of creative thought. One of our jobs as innovation leaders is to strive to understand these differences and unite and harness them in support of mission.

This chapter first touches on what philosophies motivate the individual innovator and dominate the thinking of the leaders charged with managing the innovation function at Cleveland Clinic. Next, it describes why the new locus of U.S. medical innovation is no longer industry, but our AMCs and research universities, and why it's crucial to understand and embrace this paradigm shift. Finally, it explores why convergence of the innovation philosophies in healthcare and higher education, the two bastions of mission-driven innovation, can have broad, positive effects on innovation.

An Innovator's Individual Philosophy

The concept of mission-driven innovation, as practiced by Cleveland Clinic and many of our sister institutions, is growing in understanding and gaining in popularity. What does it take to nurture it? The two main factors are presence of an innovation champion and buy-in at the top. If an organization identifies and empowers an innovation advocate, it positions itself to follow through and be successful in the practice. Furthermore, if the top executives prioritize innovation as a core value and competency, creativity will thrive.

For most physician-innovators, there's always been inspiration beyond living the Hippocratic oath, wanting to help people, and seeking financial reward. It's also the thrill of pursuing the unknown against considerable odds. I've long been inspired by the 140-word "man in the arena" excerpt from Theodore Roosevelt's 1910 speech at the Sorbonne, *Citizenship in a Republic*.

> It is not the critic who counts; not the man who points out how the strong man stumbles, or where the doer of deeds could have done them better. The credit belongs to the man who is actually in the arena, whose face is marred by dust and sweat and blood; who strives valiantly; who errs, who comes short again and again, because there is no effort without error and shortcoming; but who does actually strive to do the deeds; who knows great enthusiasms, the great devotions; who spends himself in a worthy cause; who at the best knows in the end the triumph of high achievement, and who at the worst, if he fails, at least he fails while daring greatly, so that his place shall never be with those cold and timid souls who neither know victory nor defeat.[1]

Some might judge this stance as contradictory to the disciplined, metrics-driven process of Cleveland Clinic

Innovations (CCI). How can one disengage conduct from consequence? At its heart, innovation is about "daring greatly" and is performed by those "in the arena." In a field where failure is so frequent, there must be recognition and reward for those who continue to reach and get back up when they stumble.

It's always tough and risky to be on the field, and it's easy to lob grenades from the sidelines. That's why, when working with our innovators, I make a clear distinction between *criticism* and *critical analysis*. Pure criticism diminishes all parties, while critical analysis is a requirement of the innovator leader, because it identifies shortcomings and paves the way for improvement.

Cleveland Clinic's 10 Commandments of Innovation

Over the years, a set of tenets has evolved to guide our innovation efforts. I have distilled them into these 10 commandments:

1. Innovation will occur when the most creative and qualified people are positioned for exposure to the most fertile material to inspire creative thought. This seems like a logical, almost basic concept, but it should not be taken for granted. Innovation requires the basic ingredients for the chemical reactions that produce creative outcomes. The basic substrates are need, opportunity, and ability. The catalyst may be the infrastructure that enables the development of ideas into meaningful inventions, but the pipeline is stocked by the environment that optimizes the interaction between material and makers.

2. Positioning individuals and the organization to innovate requires active strategic and structural

actions. Idea generation may seem opportunistic, but there are forces at work that enhance creativity. Whether physical, virtual, philosophical, or otherwise, a certain level of engineering can take place that improves the chances for innovation to occur. Like building a fire in the wilderness, the appropriate elements can be assembled and the opportunity to "rub two sticks together" can be enhanced with forethought by organizational leadership. Whether fostering physical proximity that helps generate breakthrough ideas, establishing policies that reward creativity, or celebrating "fast fails," the ways environments are structured influences innovation output.

3. The innovator's time for and intimacy with the commercialization process differs by individual. Optimally managing innovator involvement is a key contributor to the ultimate success of the concept. Ideas are like children, all different, and inventors are like parents, all of whom have a vested interest in their progeny's success. Some parents encourage free expression and exploration, while others hover. Similarly, some innovators choose to pass along the disclosure and return to their day jobs, while others desire a level of involvement that threatens to jeopardize execution. The innovation leader must be prepared to handle a wide spectrum of inventor involvement with education and empathy that parallels the doctor-patient relationship. Outcomes are just as rewarding when good results are achieved.

4. A commitment to best processes and best practices must be maintained by those charged with development of intellectual property (IP) for the process to

thrive and become sustainable. Innovation is a practice that relies on processes and principles. What decades ago may have been a passive function that waited for ideas and then led them down individual paths to commercialization is now a well-tested process and a highly organized journey. Although there is a great deal of consistency, there is also flexibility for customization. Achieving a balance provides sustainable success.

5. Innovation is a discipline that can be practiced, learned, taught, and measured. It has rules and requires metrics and measurement. In a dynamic environment that consistently brings new challenges and perspectives, assisting a wide spectrum of innovators and their ideas relies upon adhering to a playbook of innovation practice.

6. The benefits of innovation are realized more robustly the more closely the commercialization system is positioned to the center of the medical universe. Innovation that is destined to improve and extend human life is contributed at a prolific pace by physicians who recognize unmet needs at the bedside and then solve them. Discovery science translates into better human health more effectively when researchers are in close proximity to clinical colleagues. Creative output has a much greater chance of finding its way into the marketplace and the hands of healers if the commercialization function is closely integrated and geographically proximate to the innovators' work.

7. Innovation happens best at the intersection of knowledge domains, so seek and structure collaborations.

Many disruptive discoveries follow exposure to domains that aren't directly related. The innovation leader can catalyze interactions between creatives by orchestrating collaboration through arrangement of physical space or virtual interactions. Sometimes intellectual locks and keys reside in different places and need a little encouragement to find each other.

8. Innovation thrives best when individuals and institutions are aligned and guided by the enterprise mission. Innovation is nonlinear, fraught with failure, and long to succeed. When the innovators and their organization are aligned regarding its importance to fulfill the enterprise mission, there is intellectual freedom and there are resources to produce results, despite the risks.

9. Because of the inherent challenges associated with innovation, celebrate the pursuit and process, not just the outcome. Nothing kills innovation faster than the weight of expectation and reducing its measure of success to patents granted or dollars earned. If failure is not anticipated and even celebrated, the innovation culture will be stifled. This doesn't mean that innovation should be sloppy, wasteful, or lacking a level of expectation. But even failure has a welcome by-product, experience. While solving some of the biggest healthcare problems, stumbling is to be expected and makes eventual success that much sweeter.

10. Innovation is not the antithesis of the academic mission. It is the enabler. To some, it remains fundamentally contradictory that a commercialization function could reside within the nonprofit sector.

However, it's both an opportunity and a responsibility for the minds in healthcare to bring forth tomorrow's solutions. Success has the intended consequence of developing new revenue sources for pursuing core missions, such as patient care, further research, education, and community economic growth. With the challenges that have befallen our academic and healthcare sectors, pursuing revenue from monetizing IP is both logical and aligned with mission.

These tenets locate the ideal site for medical innovation at the center of the medical universe, where doctor and patient meet. This seems obvious to us now. But it was not always the case.

The New Locus of Medical Innovation

At Cleveland Clinic, we engage in truly "early stage" innovation—more like "earliest stage" or organic innovation. Our sweet spot is taking ideas scribbled on a napkin to first-in-man trials.

Can mission-driven innovators develop revenue-generating advances in technique and technology? Or, should innovation be isolated in large corporations with capabilities from research and development (R&D) through manufacturing, or are these too far removed from the patient's bedside to be relevant?

Cleveland Clinic advocates research *with* development. With innovation in our DNA, there were no debates on whether we should develop a commercialization and corporate venturing arm, just how we were going to build it and ensure it was aligned with our identity and mission. This has not, however, insulated us from the process of examining

scope and determining what capability should be built, partnered, or ceded to industry.

The Shift in Commercialization

Large corporations serving as the home of innovation was the
dominant model until the 1980s. But since then, there's been
a steady decline in R&D investment by industry. For the most
part, the corporate role in commercialization of innovation
is to provide the production and marketing infrastructure.
One reason for the contraction is that the risks associated
with innovation can simply be too high for the appetite of
corporate leaders and stockholders. True innovation has been
supplanted by acquisition as a means of growth in many corners of industry; this strategy is much less precarious because
revenue and customers are already established.

In addition, government's involvement influenced the
shift. Establishment of the National Science Foundation
(NSF) in 1950 and the passage by Congress of the Bayh-Dole
Act in 1980 brought about fundamental changes creating the
climate for academic innovation as we know it today. The NSF
provided a stream of research dollars to higher education, and
advancing health is among the top priorities. The Bayh-Dole
Act permitted investigators and their institutions to benefit
financially from commercialization of such research.

As a result of these developments, healthcare systems
and research universities have become the primary engines
for creative thought and have had a profound impact on the
American economy. To illustrate, in 2012 the Biotechnology
Industry Organization released *The Economic Contributions
of University/Nonprofit Inventions in the United States: 1996–
2010*. Using a decade and a half of data from the Association
of University Technology Managers (AUTM), the authors
noted that invention licensing by universities and nonprofits

during that time frame supported as many as three million person-years of employment, with a gross industry economic output as high as $836 billion.[2]

In 2011 alone, inventors at AMCs and universities earned more than $1.8 billion from commercializing their research, with royalties coming from a variety of drugs and devices. More than 12,000 new patents were filed, 5,300 licenses completed, and 617 startup companies launched, according to the annual AUTM survey.[3]

This isn't just a pendulum swing, but a profound new trajectory in innovation. It simply makes sense that innovation should initially be managed by the entities creating the ideas in the first place. Additionally, Cleveland Clinic and others feel that the fiscal benefits should also accrue to the inventor and the institution gestating the concept.

Under the prior model, IP developed at AMCs and research universities was abdicated to industry before protection or development, and inventors and their institutions or communities didn't reap the full benefits. In the new model, the institution is able to maintain control of the nascent idea and develop it. Furthermore, the ability to reward inventors with revenue from royalty-bearing licenses and spin-off companies has created novel ways to recruit and retain top talent.

The Bayh-Dole Act turned on a generous spigot that yielded breakthrough discoveries, incentivized inventors, and led to high-paying innovation-related jobs throughout the country. More than seven million U.S. jobs are directly or indirectly the result of the flourishing healthcare and bioscience sectors. In addition, governors and legislators across the country are recognizing the powerful impact that life sciences innovation can have on community economic development. This has resulted in visionary programs that provide competitive funding for creation of biotech incubators and accelerators or biotechnology clusters.

Why This *Should* Be Happening

Cleveland Clinic's broad and extensive interactions with academic colleagues have allowed us to succinctly frame innovation's role: *Innovation, and its intended commercial outcomes, does not represent the antithesis of the academic mission—it is an enabler of the academic mission.*

A tenured engineering professor at a Big 10 university and a surgery resident at Cleveland Clinic are both candidates to engage in innovation on a regular basis. Both should also be direct beneficiaries of any commercial outcomes resulting from their creative thought, and it should be shared with their institutions according to individual policies governing that activity. The benefits are compelling and do not exist at cross-purposes with the core academic mission.

What Healthcare Can Learn from Commercial Sector Innovators

The incentive to innovate is no longer simply aligned with industry's commercial or competitive inducement, but now includes multiple reasons for mission-driven institutions to engage and invest in innovation. Cleveland Clinic is often asked by other organizations how they can "get out of their own way" and take advantage of the favorable climate toward commercialization.

Here are some basic guiding topics for those embarking on their own institutional analysis.

- **Consumption, as in *consumer*.** In Cleveland Clinic's world, customers are patients. They need something that physicians uniquely dispense, in various environments that healthcare institutions typically control. Providing efficient and effective solutions that give patients a better consumer experience is one of the most promising fields of innovation. For example, in 2014 Cleveland Clinic launched AppointmentPass™, a way for patients to check in for appointments quickly, easily, and privately using a self-service electronic kiosk, similar to self check-in for an airline flight. After scheduling an appointment, patients receive via e-mail a bar code that can be printed or downloaded to a smartphone for scanning at the kiosk. The kiosk also processes insurance identification and copays. Healthcare is a service industry. Innovating around the customer—perhaps its ultimate expression—will always be the right motivation.

- **Sharing.** Because Cleveland Clinic is driven by the mission of providing better care of the sick, wherever they may be, we have taken the idea of sharing a leap forward by bringing traditional competitors together to collaborate on the supporting infrastructure required to advance innovation. For instance, Cleveland Clinic has created a Global Healthcare Innovations Alliance (GHIA), a network of healthcare systems, academic institutions, and corporate partners from around the world that collaborate to create opportunities to benefit patients through scalable technology development and commercialization.

- **Timing.** We're in the game to solve the biggest problems, regardless of how long the race. Chief among the challenges are funding gaps and the regulatory environment. Cleveland Clinic consistently endeavors to shave time from each step in our process. To help deal with allocation of scarce resources and margin pressures, we developed proprietary, multifactorial technology scoring instruments to evaluate all disclosures. While it's vital to have a filter for clinical, technical, or scientific merit, the instruments also help us make better decisions faster. We sit down with the innovator directly after the ranking session to discuss in considerable depth where the strengths and weaknesses of the contribution reside. Instead of waiting for an answer for three to six months, the innovator can resume work on the technology immediately. Use of our scoring systems has slashed our time to decision. We allocate resources better, and promising technologies reach patients faster.

- **Resourcing.** In general, most of our traditional R&D funding comes from grants or philanthropy, while commercial innovation resources come from the P&L statement or from investors expecting a return. We're balancing mission delivery with the discipline of resource management, and we're taking steps to "pay back" our funding sources, whether by turning grants into loans or tapping into the evolving venture-philanthropy ecosystem. This is a new class of philanthropists who seek high-impact investments, especially where they can measure outcome.

- **Process.** Mission-driven institutions embrace process because it's a basis for inclusion and idea sharing, while industry is more comfortable focusing on the product, its attributes, and the transactions around its dispensation. At CCI, we've made great strides by introducing technologically enabled processes into our operational infrastructure, objective mechanisms that allow us to make calls more quickly today versus five years ago. But we may give inventors the benefit of the doubt and nurture their inventions a little longer than industry typically does. Sometimes it takes more cultivating for the actual novelty and merit of an invention to shine through. We lead innovators through a more intensified filter to glean the elements of their disclosure with the greatest impact or through a remediation process that redirects creative thought down a path more suited to ultimate commercialization. There is no prescribed time limit to this process; we accommodate the clinician who has intensive patient care responsibilities or the scientist who has a grant submission deadline looming. Although we favor expediency for many reasons, such as being the first to file and achieve market primacy, we adapt our process to meet the realistic demands faced by our innovators.

- **Validation.** Mission-driven and commercial innovation share the final validation: does the innovation sell?

- **Failure.** Everyone in innovation espouses the fast, frugal failure, filtering promising solutions from the inferior as quickly (and cheaply) as possible. Failure is a real and accepted by-product of discovery. Just don't get too good at it!

Conclusion

Our universities and medical institutions will continue to be the prime locations for pioneering discovery that improves and extends human life. They will also lead in fostering the innovative culture, human capital, and connectivity necessary to form networks where researchers, entrepreneurs, investors, and manufacturers can convene and engage in vital cross-pollination that promotes successful innovation.

Members of the medical innovation ecosystem can assist the basic science researcher, engineer, or computer scientist who is contributing breakthrough scientific inquiry but does not profit from the potential commercial impact that his or her discovery might foster. Replacing the historical research and development moniker with a research *with* development mantra destigmatizes the concept of potential financial benefit from pure discovery science. Lending the process of the more mature virtuous cycle can accelerate success in the scholarly circuit.

There may be philosophical differences in the views of advocates of innovation from academia, medicine, and industry; however, there are enough similarities that, when united, can stimulate collaboration and deliver success. "I think, therefore I'm innovative" isn't a philosophy limited to one group, but can be shared, supported, and sustained by an innovation ecosystem dedicated to the mission of helping humankind and advancing knowledge.

People

Everybody Is an Innovator

Cleveland Clinic is the brains, hearts, and hands of more than 43,000 people. Our brand of mission-driven innovation is all about people, because it comes solely from people—people who have devoted their lives to making others well and to improving their results and experience.

This chapter is about how the elements we have built and collected are employed to identify, motivate, reward, and inform innovators so they can come up with new ideas to take care of patients and solve problems. It's a privilege to serve these innovators, and Cleveland Clinic Innovations (CCI) takes seriously its charge to be the caregiver of their ideas.

Mission-driven innovation parallels the doctor-patient relationship. We're entrusted with something sacred—not health in this case, but cherished ideas initiated by the inventor, who may be coming to the relationship with a variable level of understanding of the technology transfer process. Some seasoned veterans of the innovation journey are well-versed in the steps (and vicissitudes) of commercialization, while others may not have had prior exposure, or simply want to return to their "day job" and "pass the baton" to the innovation professionals. We must balance executing fiduciary responsibilities and representing the inventor with maintaining commitment to mission and representing ourselves and our institution with high integrity. *Doing well* and *doing good* embodies mission-driven innovation.

What Our Innovative People Have Done

Throughout the book, I talk about process, metrics, outcomes, and physical assets like devices or drugs. I want to share some insider information: when we describe one of the innovations we are developing on our campus, we almost always use the inventor's name, along with the technology—"That's Dr. Johnson's stent," or "Dr. Green's new molecule." Just as these groundbreaking discoveries are aimed at helping patients, they also emanate from the brilliant minds of colleagues with whom we develop intimate relationships. Both parties, the inventor and the innovations specialist, care deeply about delivering on the promise that innovation holds for mankind.

Rising from the Cleveland Clinic Fire

In May 1929, highly volatile nitrocellulose x-ray film was ignited by steam from a leaky pipe in the basement of the original Cleveland Clinic building, which still stands. The ensuing explosions and poisonous gas billowing throughout the entire building resulted in the worst fire-related disaster in the history of healthcare. Of the building's 225 occupants, 123 perished, including one of the four founders, Dr. John Phillips.

The tragedy motivated development of safety standards for hazardous material storage, improved hospital procedures, and innovations in firefighter safety and ambulance rescue.

The surviving founders leveraged their personal wealth to rebuild Cleveland Clinic and maintain operations when circulating money all but disappeared in the Great Depression.

At Cleveland Clinic, each obstacle is met with vigor and vision, every advantage is explored and exploited, every failure and challenge is pivoted for later success. Our competencies are then multiplied by the power of partnership and unanimity of thought around one mission—improving and extending human life.

Battling Colon Cancer with Computers

"You can choose your friends, but you can't choose your family," goes the old adage. But its serious side is genetically transmitted disease. If you inherit the gene for familial adenomatous polyposis, you have a 100 percent chance of developing colon cancer, and it usually manifests at younger than age 45.

Cleveland Clinic colorectal surgeon James Church collaborated with software engineer Valera Trubachev and computer scientist Elena Manilich to develop software, commercialized as Cologene, to support the largest hereditary colorectal cancer registry in the world. Not just a passive archive, Cologene has evolved into a complete decision-support and information-sharing tool. Cologene constructs family trees, coordinates testing and treatment, sets up screening plans for patients at high risk, and facilitates education. In addition, the data supports clinically important research on inherited colorectal cancer. Cologene has been lauded for ease of use, as well as robustness attributable to more than a dozen years of data collection and system enhancements.

Cologene is being used all over the world, has been translated into French and Japanese, and is available as a mobile app. Even more promising, the technology has been reconfigured to support several additional hereditary disease registries, among the world's largest.

Navigating Solutions for High-Risk Heart Patients

Imagine being able to fix heart problems while avoiding the surgical trauma of open-heart surgery, a large risk for the sickest patients. Cardiovascular surgeon José Navia recently invented a self-expandable stent and delivery system to treat mitral valve regurgitation, a disorder in which blood leaks back into the left ventricle. This serial innovator created a novel solution to the technically demanding and morbid traditional mitral valve repair that requires cracking open the chest.

His NaviGate system instead punctures a leg vein and navigates a device into the right atrium, through the septum, and down into the diseased mitral valve. Currently, the device is being tested in animal studies and is being prepared for first-in-man studies in Europe, which will be followed by U.S. clinical trials in three to five years.

Dr. Navia is among our engaged and visionary innovators who aspire to develop game-changing technologies for patients. A spin-off company, NaviGate Cardiac Structures, Inc., based on Navia's technology, has been formed to help move the innovation back to the bedside to help high-risk patients.

Everybody Is an Innovator

The innovative spirit and innate core of creativity resides in everyone. Nobody knows the job better than the person performing it. Through immersion and repetition, you find efficiencies. You associate with other experts, inside and outside of the work environment. Your vocation permeates your thoughts, and even your dreams. How many times have you been showering and you came up with an idea that made you long for pen and paper or a voice recorder? In some disciplines, you engage in scholarly discourse and contribute to the literature in your field. As such, you're in the pole position regarding what needs to be changed, can be changed, and would result from change. These are the major elements in the formula of innovation at any organization.

At Cleveland Clinic, we have developed ways to capitalize on the innovator inherent in caregivers at all levels of the institution.

Opening the Aperture as Wide as Possible

We have thousands of experts roaming an international collection of campuses—it's like a ready-made innovation laboratory where caregivers are exposed to the largest and most complex healthcare subject matter. When CCI was started, we spotted these wonderful attributes and a legacy of creative leadership. We simply had to determine how to get ideas from the bedside or lab bench to the bank to help countless others around the world. In addition, we needed to recognize that innovation was occurring in all corridors of our organization.

In the normal course of human endeavor, we often invoke axioms to help explain natural phenomena. One of the most popular is the Pareto principle—the "80-20 rule," used to describe the distribution of causes and effects.[1] However, there's a tendency to invoke the Pareto principle in evaluating sources of innovation and determining where to place resource "bets," which can translate into an artificial limitation on innovation output from an organization. There is a CCI corollary to the Pareto principle.

We've observed that when resources are scarce, institutions tend to preselect the 20 percent who they believe will contribute the most innovation and concentrate resources on them. That's not illogical—the 80-20 rule describes that 20 percent of individuals will likely contribute 80 percent of the innovations. However, we've experienced that 20 percent of those doing any job throughout the entire enterprise will be the innovators. By limiting access to innovation support by following Pareto, you artificially limit your innovation potential to 20 percent of the 20 percent. Whereas, if you follow the CCI corollary, you continue to stimulate and receive creative solutions from all corridors, and the effect of innovation success "goes viral" much faster with greater sustainability.

The reality is that when you're establishing an innovation entity like CCI, your intellectual bandwidth and human and financial resources will be stretched. Despite challenges and barriers, democratize your IP development apparatus as soon and as much as possible. Instead of focusing solely on one set of high-volume surgeons or a few well-published scientists, start with as wide an aperture as possible and never stop expanding it.

For example, the AppointmentPass™ innovation didn't come from the C-suite or even the clinical enterprise. It came from John Bona, a midlevel administrator who just thought creatively about the frustration of patients checking in for their visits.

One of the best examples of this insight about innovation potential comes from our early days working with Northwell Health (formerly North Shore-LIJ Health System), New York's largest healthcare provider and a member of the Global Healthcare Innovations Alliance (GHIA), our collaborative network of healthcare systems, academic institutions, and corporate partners.[2] Heavy, unwieldy privacy curtains separating emergency room bays in 80-plus locations frequently were wrestled down and washed in the hospital laundry. You can imagine the time-consuming manipulation of the curtains and the associated financial and environmental costs. Lorenz "Buddy" Meyer, associate director of environmental services, and Christopher Boffa, director of support services, had the idea to check the curtains for bacterial counts. They dropped to negligible levels past a narrow band at the entry aperture. Meyer and Boffa devised a vinyl panel that can be affixed to the frequently touched portion of the curtain, easily disinfected between patients, and removed and discarded when worn. This innovation was shared across our alliance, with its four large healthcare systems representing literally hundreds of emergency departments.

In short, if you want to unite a large and diverse constituency, while multiplying your organization's innovation potential, go wide *and* deep. As much as you can, open your policies and practices to everyone, not just your high earners or big name practitioners. Yes, the veteran may produce more synthetic thought than the rookie, but don't exclude the latter from the assets.

Let Ideas Speak for Themselves

One of the great characteristics of sport is that it's a meritocracy. There's an absolute measurement against which an individual's performance is judged. Your gender, race, creed, nationality, or any other personal trait doesn't influence the outcome of contests in which success is determined by how far you throw or hit, how fast you run, or how much weight you lift. Innovation shares this trait, in that the quality of an idea determines how far it goes.

Let innovative concepts speak for themselves, not the business card of origin. CCI objectified the process of innovation by developing proprietary, multivariable technology scoring instruments so that we could concentrate on the quality of the ideas. Use of these tools also disengages the inventor of origin from the technology at the decision point regarding technical or clinical merit. This helps preclude one of the fatal errors in innovation: burning scarce resources on dead-end projects because the inventor has "favored-nation" status with administration. Talented doctors and genius scientists have ideas destined for the trash bin mixed alongside their treasures. It's your job to determine which ideas have traction, not just forward all the ideas from some and disregard the promising ones from perceived lower-echelon inventors.

The intended consequence of maintaining such a disciplined methodology is the strength of decisions to kill a technology. It's exceedingly difficult to tell an inventor that his or her "baby is ugly"—that the cherished idea fails in terms of technical feasibility or market relevance. When you have proven instruments that reveal invention shortcomings, it's easier for your staff to deliver the disappointing news, plus you've identified how to possibly remediate the concept so it still has life in the commercial world.

Through broad collaboration with our alliance partners, we've undergone a small but significant change in the way we view our innovation portfolio in terms of determining absolute value. We used to see our job as finding the best ideas at *our* institution and navigating them to the marketplace. Now we believe we should simply seek the best ideas to help humankind. Wherever they grow and whoever contributes them, locate the best ideas and find a way that your organization can help shape them.

This may mean that your own institution's ideas take a subordinate role or smaller fraction. Development may result in your receiving a smaller percentage of the financial reward—so be it. If you're truly a mission-driven innovator, you realize that there are ways you can help to raise all boats by supporting the best ideas, even if they are not yours. Look for these opportunities and be prepared to stand in the shadows on some, and be cognizant of the shadows you cast when you receive the majority of the sunlight.

Just as gravity influences all bodies, the marketplace will be the ultimate arbiter of whether an innovation is worthy. It's the responsibility of innovation leadership to give an idea its best chance of survival and success. There are few disappointments greater than unrealized potential. Do everything possible to avoid this pitfall by keeping your mind and doors open to all innovators.

Carrot or Stick: Can You Make Someone More Innovative?

There is a nature-versus-nurture debate within innovation circles, just as it exists in broader society. Those who believe creativity is innate and instinctive are always poised for battle with structuralists who believe the surrounding environment is what extracts innovation.

In building Cleveland Clinic's innovation competency, we integrated the thinking of authorities Clayton M. Christensen and Tom Kelley. Two of their works focus particularly on the innovator as a person.

In Christensen's classic, *The Innovator's DNA*,[3] the modern master of disruptive thinking and his coauthors nimbly dance between arguments for innovation abilities being innate or learned. In the end, nurture trumps nature. Citing their own research and multiple replicated studies, they show that 25 to 40 percent of our innovation capacity is genetically endowed. Thus, innovation is a learned skill by a two-to-one margin. The authors identify five discovery skills, but one reigns supreme: associational thinking. Skills like "questioning, observing, networking, and experimenting" activate this capacity. But structured socialization can often determine whether disruptive innovation will result.

Kelley, in *The Ten Faces of Innovation*,[4] assigns "personalities" to the individuals and teams engaged in innovation. He articulates "learning personas," "organizing personas," and "building personas." The simplicity of Kelley's masterpiece makes it an effective tool for leading innovation. One quote that remains with me is, "The personas are about 'being' innovation rather than 'doing' innovation." Perhaps the most valuable message from *Ten Faces* is that the roles can be adopted by almost any person in an organization and then switched when opportunity or necessity arises.

These robust frameworks do a great job in identifying reproducible personal characteristics that have led to innovation or enabled leaders of innovation. However, until now in innovation literature, there were very few examples from healthcare or a mission-driven innovation perspective.

At CCI, we believe you can make somebody (or an organization) more innovative. According to Christensen, "A critical insight from our research is that one's ability to generate innovative ideas is not merely a function of the mind, but also a function of behaviors. . . . If we change our behaviors, we can improve our creative impact."[5] To "behaviors," I'd add the *environment* and *partners* that reflect or direct our behaviors, because mission-driven innovation is such a team game.

When addressing groups from other academic medical centers who've asked CCI to help them evaluate preparedness for innovation, I often ask, "How many of you are innovators?" Even clarifying that I didn't say *inventors*, I'm still shocked with the paltry show of hands.

CCI eventually figured out why our constituents were so ill-prepared to classify themselves as innovators: they lack creative boundaries, innovation infrastructure, and rewards. We held a mirror up to this set of problems to distill the transformative elements: calibrating creative focus, participating in a structured innovation process, and participating in reward related to creative thought.

Calibrating Creative Focus

We're all problem solvers. In both our personal and professional lives, we identify and rectify challenging situations multiple times a day. These are the hurdles right in front of us, sometimes demanding our full attention. Even if somewhat out of the ordinary in content, they're usually defined in scope and timing.

The reason some individuals fail to engage in innovation is that it lacks boundaries. The grand challenges, such "cure cancer" or "provide better healthcare in third-world countries" are just too expansive, even for the most capacious thinkers. Innovation leaders can address this barrier by helping their colleagues learn focus around creative thought.

Innovation by limitation sounds like an oxymoron. But it is helpful to remind the creative individual that "eating the elephant one bite at a time" is often the only way to accomplish the most daunting tasks. Innovators naturally feel limited by the encroachment of their "day jobs" or even the anticipated length of their careers. We can assist them by steering them toward manageable projects or elements thereof, then introducing the power of innovation partnerships.

Participating in a Structured Innovation Process

Every time we bring in a new member of our GHIA and provide access to our structured innovation function, there's a flood of pent-up disclosures. The problem identification and creative solution wheels were turning, but the assessment and development function was missing from the new partner's innovation milieu.

For example, MedStar Health, our first global alliance partner, registered no disclosures from its nearly 25,000 caregivers in 2010. During its first full year of operation in 2011, our alliance tracked 111 disclosures. Our friends at MedStar didn't become innovative all of a sudden. The switch got flipped when the organization was made aware of the process.

We still debate whether simply having a robust innovation capability makes individuals or an organization more innovative. We subscribe to the belief and practice that you can stimulate meaningful innovation—not by simple reward and certainly not by looming penalty for those who do not take part in idea development. Basically, it is through extraction of the innate creative capability by surrounding it with the apparatus that innovation is augmented. But without infrastructure, not much progress will be made.

We have found that you must make your constituents aware of the innovation apparatus that is available to them. It is too easy to "default" to subjugating new ideas when the rigors of the day intercede. Educating your talented creatives about the services available to them overcomes the initial attrition of potentially promising concepts.

Participating in Reward Related to Creative Thought

There may be no more hotly contested debates in academic innovation than whether innovators should be rewarded for creative contributions—and if rewarded, by what mechanism. Summarized below are some of the key realities. Several are contentious and will receive more attention.

- No inventor reward policy is mandated by law in either the private or public sector.

- Under U.S. law, all patents are considered owned initially by the inventor; however, prevailing employment agreements often assign intellectual property (IP) rights to the employer.

- The assignment mechanism and the reach of the employer into the creative work of its employees outside of the employment environment are determined by individual policy and contract.

- The reward policy is likewise determined between the employer and its innovator-employees.

- The concept of reward varies—monetary compensation is the most obvious inducement, but advancement (including academic tenure) is also considered a form of innovation reward.

- Institutions variously value innovations that reach different stages of maturity—for example, disclosure, patent application, granted patent, and commercialization.

- Financial rewards include, but are not limited to, internal bonuses or prizes for innovation competitions, royalties from licenses, and company equity.

- A growing number of academic organizations celebrate their inventors with campus-based ceremonies, plaques, banquets, etc.

- Many institutions, including Cleveland Clinic, struggle with determining whether an innovation was developed in the normal course of executing the employee's vocational responsibilities.

- There's both an academic and a practical debate whether financial reward creates incentive or disincentive for innovation.

Innovation Versus Expectation

While each of these 10 realities deserves attention, the final two create the majority of debate and are the most ambiguous. The Pareto principle strikes again!

Accepting the assumption that everyone's an expert and has the capability to innovate, it follows that both incremental improvement and disruptive advancement will result from normal daily work. The innovation leader is challenged with how to recognize and reward the innovation that stems from the inventor's "day job."

Whether an innovation is eligible for compensation according to institutional inventor policies is often determined by one test—was the idea conceived (and built) during the individual's vocational engagement. This determination is not always straightforward at Cleveland Clinic and often requires adjudication by our Innovations Governance Advisory Board. Let's recount three common situations:

Scenario A: Mary Jones, an orthopaedic surgeon, develops a new implant to stabilize fractures, resulting in a patent-protected device. A large manufacturer purchases the license for the implant, and royalties are negotiated. Dr. Jones's real job is to see patients and do surgery. Although she may have been stimulated or inspired by the clinical material she encountered during her job, she was not originally hired to develop next-generation device solutions. The result is that Dr. Jones can participate in the upside, according to Cleveland Clinic's inventor and distribution guidelines (40 percent of the net proceeds of any divestment and ongoing payment stream, with no limit on the absolute amount or the time over which the inventor receives rewards).

Scenario B: Bill Johnson works in the office of the CFO. He is tasked with developing new software to gather and analyze patient billing data. Due to his position, Bill controls institutional funds that he directed into accelerating the project. These software advancements would not be classified as an innovation for which the creator would receive direct financial consideration. Bill could get rewarded through our annual performance review process or some other institutional recognition, but would not participate in a royalty or equity position. His case is even clearer because he was able to direct funds to a project, usually an automatic disqualification from participating in revenue streams.

Scenario C: Jack Green is a postdoctoral fellow in the bioengineering lab and also participates in co-innovation with Dr. Jones, our orthopaedic surgeon. Dr. Green is expert with the prototyping machines on which Dr. Jones's new implants were developed, and he made the first 5 to 10 mock-ups. He suggested a slight modification that ultimately was incorporated. In this case, Dr. Green was acting in a technical support role, which would not qualify him to receive remuneration. Where it gets more challenging is determining whether his scholarly contribution substantively influenced the design of the implant. Our rule of thumb is that if the individual has contributed enough to be listed on the patent, then he or she probably deserves financial consideration for the intellectual components.

The Influence of Rewards on Innovation

Cleveland Clinic's inventor distribution policy is a 60-40 split of net proceeds of a commercial license. Inventors receive 40 percent, while the remaining 60 percent is equally divided between the inventor's clinical institute of origin, CCI, and Cleveland Clinic's Lerner Research Institute.

This distribution scheme clearly recognizes the contribution of the inventor. Obviously if there's co-innovation, the primary innovator(s) are determined. The 20 percent to our research institute was designed to recognize the contribution discovery scientists make to most advances. Despite some projects developing without influence from our research infrastructure, the research institute remains worthy of our support, especially in today's challenged fiscal environment.

There's no misperception that all innovation happens in the off-hours. Physicians, scientists, executives, and others rarely turn off their brains, so substantial innovation is being accomplished during office hours or operating room block time. Instead of quibbling about how much light, heat, and water an innovator may have utilized while ideating, or insisting upon a time accounting of when ideas were conceived or developed, compensating the unit of the innovator's origin has proven highly successful for us. Usually, institute leadership deploys the monies received to perpetuate the innovation infrastructure, specifically by providing seed funding to emerging projects and participating in committees that screen innovation merit.

There are some who argue against financial rewards for innovation in an academic setting.[6] The prevailing sentiments range from apprehension about misjudging the value of creative thought by existing standards to more theoretical concern about contaminating the academic mission with financial inducement. It may be valid that incentives are built around what we already know and understand how to measure. But our viewpoint is that reward for innovation activity enables rather than contradicts the academic mission.

To date, CCI has distributed over $90 million to on-campus inventors. According to our IP and inventor policies, we have no maximum to the distribution, nor does the time during which an inventor may benefit from his or her invention expire. We write six- and seven-figure checks to our inventors and have never regretted our policy. This motivates not only the recipients but also those around them to continue to pursue innovation.

We are all on one-year contracts at Cleveland Clinic, and there is no bonus structure. We do get compensation adjustments after the annual performance review, but those follow for only another year. The ability to enhance independent wealth generation by participating in royalty-bearing licenses or equity stakes in companies created from ideas is a strong differentiator that attracts and retains top talent in Cleveland. It's gratifying to be a master clinician in itself, but when one adds the role of inventor, job satisfaction increases.

Every year, CCI bestows the F. Mason Sones Award for outstanding contribution in healthcare innovation. Examples of winning innovations include Vincent K. Tuohy for breast cancer vaccine research and Irene Katzan for development of our Knowledge Program, a new way to integrate patient feelings and outcomes into the electronic medical record. The Sones award is accompanied by a $50,000 check presented at our CEO's annual State of the Clinic address to employees. Judging by the growing number of nominations, this mechanism also increases the awareness of and participation in innovation.

The tenured environment presents difficulties in terms of incentives for innovation. Measures such as number of papers, grants, or graduate students mentored can be tracked and weighed in tenure decisions. But how about contribution of groundbreaking technology with positive cultural and commercial outcomes? There's growing appreciation that innovation resulting in commercialization should be considered in tenure decisions. While Cleveland Clinic is not an institution that grants tenure, many institutions like the University of Pennsylvania or our GHIA partner, the University of Notre Dame, are bringing innovation into the tenure discussion.[7]

Combating the Tyranny of Sequential Activity

I often ask inventors why they consistently pursue new solutions, while I simultaneously assess my own motivations. The answers are rarely about remuneration; innovators seek significance more than success. Attempting to synthesize the answers, I repeatedly hear about the primary frustration that almost every physician experiences during his or her career: We can care for only one patient at a time. I've heard this called the tyranny of sequential activity.

Once you've achieved a certain level of experience and expertise, you feel a responsibility to share it as widely as you can. That's just how most colleagues think about distributing the gifts they've been given to help people. One way to extend yourself is geographically; many noble colleagues do mission work or practice in underserved areas. Unfortunately, even these individuals are still limited by the tyranny of sequential activity once they arrive at their destinations around the corner or around the world.

The alternative for physician-inventors is immersion in the challenges and rewards of innovation. Although they may be capable of touching only a limited number of patients in a day—those right in front of them—some instrument, device, or technique they create may touch dozens or hundreds around the world.

Contributing IP that can be scaled and distributed is the way to multiply yourself. It's like dispensing knowledge through books or exposing larger communities to music through recordings. Inventing techniques and technologies that put capability in the hands of trained colleagues worldwide is one of the most rewarding things you can be engaged in.

The greatest satisfaction for my co-innovators comes from the highly personal and unique gratification that comes from multiplying themselves by mastering scalability.

One of my favorite Appalachian aphorisms is, "When you go to the fancy-dress ball, you dance with who brung ya." There's a pearl in that statement about the value of loyalty, but another interpretation is to stick with the set of attitudes and aptitudes that got you this far. In the field of innovation, it means that people will likely contribute in their particular field of specialty, so do everything in your power to surround them with infrastructure and interaction.

When your creatives start wandering off into territory that belongs to others and their ideas are consistently off the mark, nudge them back to doing what they do best, to "dance with who brung 'em."

Building the Cleveland Clinic Team

At CCI, we seek ultimate team players who have the capability to be team captain. We seek individual high achievers with a deep commitment to advancing the art and science of both medicine and the process of innovation.

Another required trait is unwavering service orientation. It's not an understatement that inventors think about their ideas consistently, some constantly. As an inventor myself, I am equally guilty, knowing personally how often my wheels were turning about some minute detail of an invention disclosure or where my submission was in the development or transaction process. Managing hundreds of inventors requires people passionate about facilitating the arduous path from bedside or lab bench to bank.

Of course, all of our interactions hinge on adept communication skills. This may range from distilling sophisticated business terms for a scientist to delivering bad news about finding prior art that bursts another innovator's bubble to involvement in a delicate negotiation over equity or investment for a first-time inventor.

Our colleagues at CCI are seasoned professionals, with the insight and capability to divine the merit of ideas in absolute terms, while considering the attractiveness to investors or market impact of the fully formed offerings that may result. We sometimes jest that the best candidate for a position at CCI holds MD, PhD, JD, and MBA degrees and is a notary public. Frankly, now that we have many team members who hold several or most of those degrees, it's no longer a joke!

Once a group is assembled, instincts take over that are similar to those who are creating championship organizations. The best coaches know where to place individuals to bring about both individual and team success. I credit CCI's senior leadership with much of the insight that has placed our stars in positions in which they can excel, while ensuring there are robust professional development pathways.

Not all players have the same gifts; shortstops have a different skill set from pitchers or catchers. While the same holds true in the innovation business, I'm consistently impressed with how proficient everyone at CCI is as a utility infielder. They may have deep domain or industry experience, but they are sufficiently open-minded and flexible to provide insight across our portfolio.

This invokes Kelley's "I-shaped versus T-shaped" people concept from *The Ten Faces of Innovation*.[8] Kelley captures what most of us innately recognize: that there are people who achieve a level of expertise and success but limit themselves to their domain of engagement. These he calls I-shaped people. There's absolutely nothing wrong with that. In fact, it really reflects one of the strengths of vertically oriented care-delivery systems like Cleveland Clinic. Extreme focus allows extraordinary expertise.

You can't imagine how many times I was the butt of jokes about whether I operate on only the right hand or the left, because hand surgeons are known for being super-sub-subspecialists. It's a luxury to explore the depths of one pursuit, but it does have a drawback: it can prevent the type of benefits that come from connectivity or association.

While we don't exactly advocate the jack-of-all-trades philosophy, we do see the merit of the "T-shaped" person, who has deep domain expertise permitting understanding of intricacies and who maintains a current Rolodex of key players in the related development, investment, regulatory, and legal fields. And although such an individual may be the medical-device development guru, he or she also knows what's going on in pharma or health information technology (HIT). This is especially relevant, because some deals have elements that directly overlap, especially with HIT, which seems to touch almost everything.

The additive effect of cross-pollination, so important in organic innovation, is precisely why the professionals of CCI inhabit a singular facility. The benefit is the water-cooler conversations that facilitate information exchange and the final puzzle pieces being found from sources outside the domain work group. The other thing that hiring T-shapers does is foster respect among colleagues—they come to understand that others face and surmount similar challenges. Help on a deal may be no further than two offices over.

Of course, we don't rely only on chance meetings when our mavens get dehydrated. One of the most important tools is our quarterly business review (QBR). During the QBR, each of our domain incubators (medical device, therapeutics and diagnostics, HIT, and delivery solutions) presents its in-progress deals. Technologies and commercialization or investment approaches are detailed. We walk away from the QBRs with deep respect for the capabilities of teammates and usually leave with something clarified or with leads in our own spheres.

The QBR is also the time when we discuss our strategies for CCI. All teams work best when communication is at its most robust, and CCI is no exception. When we have our entire roster of colleagues gathered, we get the chance to reaffirm our core mission, while also revealing where we believe the puck is going. We follow with a completely open Q&A session. This level of transparency is one of the elements that accelerate innovation, while enfranchising our valuable contemporaries.

We're also sure to celebrate successes at the QBRs. Recognizing triumphs publically has a favorable effect on individuals who participate directly in the achievement and sends a message that we rejoice in the good fortune of others. Everybody in the room anticipates when they'll next share the spotlight. We don't avoid critical analysis during these sessions, but we lean much more toward positive public recognition of teams and instead deal with individual challenges in more private settings.

Our "minor-league" development mechanism is our internship program. This structured experience brings energetic and intelligent young men and women to CCI for three or four months and is heavily oversubscribed each year. We hire over a dozen promising scholars, ranging from high schoolers to those about to graduate from JD/MBA programs, who have a keen interest in innovation and entrepreneurship.

Interns are the gift you give yourself. All of us need to replenish our energy, thoughts, and enthusiasm. Frankly, it also doesn't hurt to be reminded that your job is cool and attractive to the best and brightest coming up through the ranks. We get as much as we give to the interns. Because they're unencumbered by the scar tissue of failures or seemingly insoluble problems, interns can provide insight that breaks stalemates and defuses standoffs.

You must allow interns a voice. When you carry the same title in medical training, you inhabit the lowest rung and aren't really called upon to provide more than the fruits of perspiration, not inspiration. When life and death are at stake, seasoned professionals sometimes don't want to waste time and energy on the opinions of those not yet acculturated in the field.

We look at it a little differently. The intern probably spent considerable time with the inventor, heard from every consultant, and had just enough knowledge to discern the nomenclature, but not so much that bias crept in. The intern is precisely the person to ask, "What's the next step?" or simply, "What do you think?" Listen to them. They're often the closest to the action and, if made to feel comfortable, could provide critical insight into inventors and industry.

We've hired a great many of our interns. They get to know our people and our culture. They've taken the time to learn what mission-driven innovation is and to understand its intricacies. They're as enthusiastic about the pursuit as the product. They remind us how important it is to teach and live innovatively.

I conclude with a simple reality of managing people: Your staff will be recruited by other organizations—some will move on. What else would you expect when you've attracted bright and creative people, then tasked them with critical responsibilities on which they performed splendidly?

We've seen executives take one of two roads in dealing with that eventuality. Some immediately assume that an employee entertaining an attractive job offer is disloyal, while others celebrate that their people are sought after because of their contribution to a leading organization. Take the high road.

Besides the fact that we should all rejoice in the good fortune of others, the innovation community is a "small dance floor"; we have an interdependence and level of connectivity that puts us in frequent, if not constant, contact. I'm so proud of our team at CCI and truly believe that, as servant leaders, we work for them, not the inverse. However, we're also proud that former CCI employees now head the innovation functions at Johns Hopkins University, Partners Healthcare, and Vanderbilt University. Just as a university or residency training program celebrates the accomplishments of graduates because the diaspora expands the scope and identity of the alma mater, Cleveland Clinic has become known as the cradle of innovation leaders.

There is no shortage of good ideas. It's a noble pursuit to empower and align the most experienced professionals in the industry to develop and divest them. This dedication brings personal success, honors institutional identities, and helps patients. In the final analysis, it's good to remember that it wasn't just the drug or device that helped the patient. It was also an innovator—a person who cared deeply and leveraged intellect and skill to positively influence the lives of others.

Process

*"Our need for rules does not arise from
the smallness of our intellects, but from
the greatness of our task. Discipline is
not necessary for things that are slow and
safe: but discipline is necessary for things
that are swift and dangerous"*

—G.K. CHESTERTON

The Importance of
Innovation Infrastructure

Effective process is the singular asset that differentiates a
creative institution from an innovative one. Unequivocally,
this is where the rubber meets the road. An operational
commercialization or technology-transfer infrastructure is
the foundation for building a high-innovation environment.
It's the absolute minimum investment an organization can
make to play in the contemporary sphere of modern mission-
driven innovation.

In the linear flow of product development that pervades most commercial markets, engineers try to predict market migration or "experts" use data from focus groups to predict consumer demand. The medical innovation journey, however, begins at the bedside or laboratory bench. An engaged caregiver recognizes an unmet need and draws upon his or her talents to address it. Then it's incumbent upon the institutional innovation infrastructure to develop and divest the creative solution to return it to the clinician. This is the virtuous cycle.

Mastering the multi-step process by which technologies are gestated in this virtuous cycle revolving around the patient is both a challenge and an opportunity for newly emerging mission-driven innovation organizations. Details of how Cleveland Clinic Innovations (CCI) developed and operates its virtuous cycle—its commercialization infrastructure—are revealed in this chapter.

The success of such a model, and its major distinguishing characteristic from pure academic idea generation usually associated with research universities, is that the marketing is already done on the front end. Most of my colleagues have engaged in research and contributed robustly to discovery science, so we don't diminish pursuit of "ideas for the sake of ideas," but we're sticking with our definition of innovation as meaning the process by which ideas are put to work.

The Virtuous Cycle: The Foundation of Mission-Driven Innovation

To participate in innovation today, an organization must invest in—or access through partnership—people and practices dedicated to operating healthcare innovation's virtuous cycle. (See Figure 4.1.) A virtuous cycle, or circle, is the term used to describe a complex chain of related events or steps,

FIGURE 4.1 The Virtuous Cycle

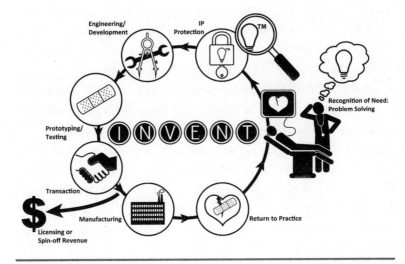

involving strong expertise and engagement and compounding in a positive feedback loop. When operated optimally, it's the opposite of the vicious circle, or cycle, a comparable set of recurring events that conspire to spin out of control and result in negative consequences.

We developed commercialization competencies and infrastructure early and robustly, and then grew them in a dynamic manner over the past two decades. While our earliest efforts were driven mainly by enthusiasm and old-fashioned trial and error, we quickly realized the necessity of approaching innovation with the same seriousness of purpose as establishing a new clinical program. We assembled the key players, mapped our needs, analyzed our capability, and designed a road map to become a leader.

We also developed disciplined processes so that inventors, investors, and market partners knew where they stood. A great deal of innovation administration relies on trust, which is the by-product of honest exchange, expectation setting, and delivery of the promised outcome or an honest explanation of failure. Only a disciplined engagement can yield such trust. Cleveland Clinic's virtuous cycle evolved gradually, honed by repetition in handling thousands of new ideas.

Some of the more pertinent elements of our virtuous cycle include: (1) structured ideation engagements; (2) processes for handling of disclosure; (3) disciplined filters to identify viable and nonviable ideas; (4) development of metrics and monitoring milestones; and (5) engagement with advisors and deal makers. Key roles are also played by experienced legal, engineering, and regulatory professionals; these resources are integral to the operation of a world-class commercialization engine.

The virtuous cycle is easy to describe but challenging to erect and execute. Its success is first predicated on proximity to a wellspring of idea generation, the innovators that provide the raw material. At Cleveland Clinic, transformative concepts don't emanate just from the physicians and research scientists, but from literally every corridor and echelon of the organization. This is why open access to the innovation apparatus is so critical. Cleveland Clinic's advantage in stimulating widespread creative thinking is clear—an expert, often *the* world expert, recognized an unmet need and provided the makings of a solution.

The journey toward the marketplace, however, is a long one, during which the idea will take many forms. Within the virtuous cycle is a linear progression of those ideas toward commercialization, and the step that completes the cycle is when the innovation is returned to the inventor's hands.

We coined an easily remembered acronym, INVENT, to cover the steps and events in the virtuous cycle. (See Figure 4.2.) Both seasoned and blossoming inventors have embraced the INVENT concept as a way to understand how

FIGURE 4.2 Cleveland Clinic Innovations' INVENT
Commercialization Process

successful ideas progress through the typical commercialization milestones.

- **Idea submission.** An innovator completes our formal web-based Invention Disclosure Form (IDF), which describes the novel concept. The IDF (see Appendix A) is the basis for presentation of the idea to a clinical or administrative-specific Peer Review Committee (PRC).

- **Need assessment.** A PRC evaluates the clinical, scientific, and/or technical merit of the disclosure and considers and scores its ability to affect practice. High-scoring disclosures are passed on for evaluation of commercial potential.

- **Viability assessment.** Endorsement from the PRC leads to attention from seasoned business leaders and staff advisors in the appropriate domain incubators. For Cleveland Clinic, these are medical devices, therapeutics and diagnostics, health information technology (HIT), and delivery solutions. A business case for the invention is prepared by domain experts, and an internal leadership group, the CCI Steering Committee, designs a path forward to the market for investors.

- **Enhancement.** A development plan for the invention is prepared and executed. We reach out to the market to garner interest and gather relevant feedback. The commercialization strategy is refined by members of our Innovation Advisory Board (IAB), and inventions are marketed.

- **Negotiation.** Negotiations are initiated with interested corporate partners or investors. Decisions regarding the concept's ultimate form, royalty-bearing license or spin-off company (NewCo), are made.

- **Translation.** The original idea emerges on the commercial stage. Although operational responsibilities typically now fall to the licensee or NewCo operator, CCI usually maintains a governance role and monitors the licenses.

For more information on the INVENT Process, visit http://innovations.clevelandclinic.org/Inventor/Commercialization-Process.aspx#.VWM96VVVhBc.

The Virtuous Cycle Meets the Scholarly Circuit

Although we work with many for-profit companies that seek to understand and integrate medical innovation into their portfolios, we have long associated with sister organizations in the nonprofit sector—AMCs and research universities. An increasing number now embrace the so-called *virtuous cycle* of innovation that has been so advantageous for bringing life science and/or biotechnology advances to the marketplace.

Cleveland Clinic is chief among the pioneers and practitioners of the virtuous cycle. The answers to tomorrow's medical challenges are identified by innovators engaged at the forefront of care and research, and developed in-house by those institutions that have built infrastructures to gestate ideas into commercialized outcomes. From the protection of intellectual property (IP) to the core engineering or coding activities and development of the investment/divestment relationships, these functions can now be handled by the same hospital or institution of higher learning from which the innovations originated.

The shift in innovation locus from industry to the AMC means a corresponding shift in the relationship between hospitals and corporations. We no longer simply engage in the sale of commercially engineered wares. Instead, the marketplace is increasingly coming to hospitals and academic institutions to obtain our product lines. A swelling portfolio of homegrown technologies is now developed at the same institutions at which they were discovered.

What makes it a cycle is that ultimately the idea takes the form of commercialized products (devices, drugs, or software solutions) that are returned to the hands of the inventors. The creators or their clinical colleagues employ the products at the patient's bedside to improve and extend human life.

The Next Step in Evolution

As a pioneer in commercialization, Cleveland Clinic has been active in discerning the next step in bringing ideas from the bedside and laboratory bench back to caregivers' hands to help patients. It's merging the innovation philosophies of AMCs and research universities to work better together on society's healthcare challenges. Each party brings valuable components, and each can be equally rewarded.

While universities typically pursue knowledge for the sake of expanding understanding, AMCs start with a

FIGURE 4.3 The Scholarly Circuit

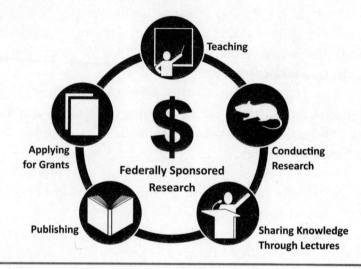

problem and then bring to bear one or more expert minds to find the solution. The scholarly circuit moves on to share knowledge through presentations and publications. But according to the virtuous cycle within AMCs such as Cleveland Clinic, publication or public presentation is done *after* the IP has been secured, so that disseminated sharing doesn't negate the ability to patent or otherwise protect our IP.

In the scholarly circuit, the holy grail of funding—from federal sources, special-interest funders, or philanthropists—starts another cycle. Regardless of the source, the goal is the funding itself, because it enables another trip around the circle, as depicted in Figure 4.3.

A perfect storm of funding challenges is clouding the scholarly circuit. Let's start with the biggie: federal funding for scholarly research is becoming scarcer, both decreasing and shifting away from basic and applied research toward some form of translational research. Additionally, healthcare

FIGURE 4.4 Uniting the Virtuous Cycle and the Scholarly Circuit

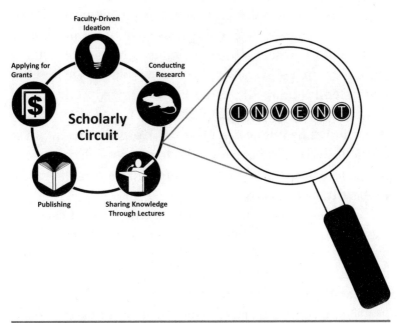

reform has put pressure on hospital discretionary income, thus threatening research support. All of this is occurring at a time when industry's investment in its own R&D is on the decline.

Can the more seasoned medical innovation process translate academic research into commercial outcomes? The result would be a win-win. The research accrues to the common good, and the funding gap is closed through revenue from commercialization.

What we suggest is akin to taking academic research to medical (innovation) school. Continue to celebrate discovery science, but amplify research *with* development approaches. Promote the liaison between the virtuous cycle and the scholarly circuit, while introducing industry as a trusted partner for funding and unmet need identification (Figure 4.4).

Tapping into the circuit at the appropriate time would align with mission-driven innovation in two ways: (1) by bringing the perspective of the healthcare-based innovation ecosystem to evaluate the developing technologies residing within research universities, more novel solutions to improve and extend human life could be recognized and pointed toward directly helping people; and (2) before patentability is precluded by public disclosure, the sophistication of the virtuous cycle could be employed to maximize commercial outcome, delivering additional sources to supplement grants to sustain the scholarly circuit.

The benefits are many and distributed. The medical innovation ecosystem would gain previously unavailable visibility into ideas evolving on university campuses that could cure diseases, and a new source of revenue could offset the decline in federally funded research dollars.

To summarize our key assertions about the university-based scholarly circuit and academic healthcare's virtuous cycle:

- Healthcare innovation's virtuous cycle has tended to realize more robust commercialization outcomes than the scholarly circuit.

- Unprecedented funding pressures may be the catalyst for the two systems to find ways to work together productively to increase commercial outcome from research activity—research *with* development.

- These models should be relatively facile to optimize by uniting them at a key stage of idea development— before ideas are publically shared in a manner that would negate patent protection.

- Federal policy (the Bayh-Dole Act) is already in place to reward both members; alignment and execution of institutional policy could unite the virtuous cycle and the scholarly circuit for the benefit of both parties, their communities, and the patients they serve.

Identifying, accepting, and addressing these realities is the first step in preparing the larger innovation ecosystem to withstand the pressures that will be applied to it in the new millennium. It paves the way for a convergence of the basic philosophies that allows ideas to become both intellectual and commercial successes. Ultimately, it doesn't detract from, but adds to, the ability of the healthcare system to further its mission.

At its core, CCI is a service function. Our commercialization process provides professional amenities to inventors to develop and divest their IP. The lessons learned from managing assets as precious as a person's ideas, especially ones that may save lives, are valuable. Dynamic effort should always be directed toward mastering each step, then aggregating the expertise into a reproducible practice, thus the virtuous cycle.

It is noble to transport an idea from the moment it sparked in the innovator's mind back to his or her hands to eradicate suffering. The distinguishing characteristic that allowed CCI to pioneer the leading innovation function in healthcare was identifying and internalizing the key steps in the virtuous cycle. The operation and outcome of this function is completely aligned with our mission. The efficiencies and experience we placed within our walls has become another distinguishing characteristic of our enterprise and is as integral to our fabric as our dedication to patient care, scientific inquiry, and teaching.

An example of the level and impact of commercialization services that CCI provides is the recent new company ImageIQ. Most of the IP commercialized to date by CCI has been aimed at fulfilling Cleveland Clinic's mission of providing better care of the sick. ImageIQ, a 2011 spin-off, addresses another mission pillar: investigation into their problems.

ImageIQ supports clinical research and drug and medical device trials with cutting-edge image analysis and software technology. Its advanced and powerful tools can combine, analyze, and objectively interpret anything from microscopic slides to visible light pictures. Whether it's 2-D, 3-D, or 4-D, ImageIQ technology is capable of reducing what it sees to quantifiable scientific measurements.

Capabilities were developed and refined over a decade in Cleveland Clinic's Lerner Research Institute and Biomedical Imaging and Analysis Center. Realizing the technology's commercialization promise, CCI provided initial funding from its Global Cardiovascular Innovation Center (GCIC) incubator—and everything from phone and Internet service to physical space and bouncing ideas off other smart people, which allowed the entrepreneurs to focus solely on the emerging business.

The company started with four employees but now has more than a dozen. It relies heavily on software experts and found the talent it needed locally, thanks to the area's many universities and software businesses. ImageIQ's initial markets were envisioned to be medical devices, pharmaceutical, and research organizations, but other sectors, including agricultural science, industrial manufacturing, and behavioral sciences, are showing excitement.

ImageIQ moved to a stand-alone building in 2014 and launched two new product lines in early 2015, an imaging-enabled electronic data capture and management system for drug and device clinical trials and a cloud-based preclinical image analysis website.

Step 1: Engage Innovators Through Education

To access innovators' creative hard drives and software, we stewards of innovation not only must set the culture, we must ensure that we've cultivated awareness of what innovation is and how it works. We must build rapport and trust with the inventors to make them not only comfortable but eager to turn their ideas over to a function in which they have confidence.

The first stake you drive when you're building your institution's innovation platform is inventor outreach. Identify members of the innovator pool, get their attention, engage their ambition, and teach them the innovation protocols. We accomplished this through a structured program of Inventors Forums that cycle annually. Never meant to replace one-on-one connection between CCI and the inventor, these sessions are the boot camp where intellectual creatives become innovators and the ingenious become inventive. Some 250 to 300 participants typically attend.

Our forums are the "grand rounds" of innovation, ensuring that all the basics are covered and our colleagues are level set on information and expectation. The tricky part is also providing enough depth that veteran innovators get credits toward their innovation "doctorates." At minimum, there's enough change in patent law, venture investment trends, institutional IP policy, and regulatory standards that refreshers are always warranted.

We typically kick off in May, National Inventors Month. The sessions are 90 minutes long and mix didactic elements with case examples and generous question-and-answer segments. The faculty is composed of CCI staff, successful inventors from the institution, and outside luminaries who bring unique viewpoints. The sessions are videotaped and made available on Cleveland Clinic's intranet for later viewing. The sidebar features examples of our annual Inventors Forum topics and session descriptions.

CLEVELAND CLINIC INVENTORS FORUM TOPICS

How Do I INVENT?

Cleveland Clinic is celebrating National Inventors Month. Join us as we honor all active and aspiring inventors by hosting an Inventors Forum on what it takes to innovate in the new era of healthcare. Attendees will hear from Cleveland Clinic Innovations (CCI) leadership about our new INVENT process and get to know our innovation managers and incubator directors. Attendees will then hear from a panel of Cleveland Clinic inventors.

Global Impact: Delivering Innovations to Patients via Licenses or Startups

Once your innovation has run the INVENT gauntlet of idea submission, need and viability assessment, and enhancement, it's now time to negotiate with companies and investors to translate the invention into a patient-benefiting product or company. In this session, CCI experts will discuss the decision criteria for licensing a technology or launching a new company, negotiation nuances between licensees and investors, and what it takes to finally execute a deal. Attendees will then hear from seasoned Cleveland Clinic inventors who will give firsthand accounts of what to expect once your invention is in the market.

Enhancing Your Invention

For an invention to make it to market, it not only needs to be sketched, it needs to be built, tested, and packaged.

While innovating on your own can be expensive, CCI works with inventors every day to identify proper funding channels and expedient resources to get inventions across the finish line. In this forum, experts will discuss these various avenues, as well as provide tips for strategically innovating in our current value-based climate.

Planting Your Flag

A common misperception of innovation is that it starts and ends with patents. In reality, there are many ways to protect an invention. We will discuss the dos and don'ts of protecting medical devices, therapeutics and diagnostics, HIT, and delivery solutions, illustrated by real-life case studies from the annals of innovation at many companies throughout history. The forum will also give an overview of the U.S. Patent and Trademark Office's (USPTO) recent implementation of the first-to-file law.

The Evaluation, Enhancement, and Marketing of Your Invention

Does your invention have what it takes? In this session, we'll look at how to go from ideation to commercial innovation. We'll talk about the journey through the INVENT process, what each step entails, and who is involved along the way in order to bring your product to market. The forum will also feature members of the Innovation Advisory Board (IAB), who will discuss its role, provide an overview of the current commercial landscape, and underscore the benefits of working with our incubators on key innovations.

The goal of robust and recurring educational modules is to connect the individual's creative DNA with the structured ideation and process orientation of the contemporary innovation practice. Many inventors simply want to turn over their IP to the CCI function, while others insist on step-by-step updates and want to know when even incremental progress is made at any of the germinal stages. The next section lifts up the hood so the reader can see inside the process at its most intimate detail.

Step 2: Importance of Filters

You might be surprised to learn the most frequent complaint from innovators about their institution's commercialization apparatus. It's not hearing that their "baby is ugly," our euphemism that an idea is unoriginal, inadequate, or uninvestable. Instead, it's ambiguity and delay regarding outcome. And nothing damages an innovator's spirit more than being in a perpetual state of uncertainty.

Three variables typically contribute to ambiguity: delay in communication of the outcome; belief that the idea was evaluated by individuals of lesser expertise than the inventor; and lack of clear reasoning or methodology for rejection of the concept.

Just as you can't blame inventors for illiteracy in the language of innovation, they also can't be expected to comprehend the economics. We all inherently understand the concept of allocation of scarce resources, but when inventors believe they have the next cure for cancer, the dollars and cents just don't seem overly relevant to them. This is precisely why an initial filter that yields a reliable predictor of success is one of the most valuable tools the innovation function can maintain.

To satisfy the three "anti-ambiguity" criteria we set forth, CCI constructed a best process that has become best practice, our Peer Review Committees. They evolved from an earlier mechanism to evaluate the clinical relevance and technical or scientific merit, the Commercialization Council, which operated from the earliest days of CCI. Let's compare and contrast the two approaches to emphasize what we believe to be the contemporary standard for launching the initial stage of the virtuous cycle that occurs right after disclosure.

To be clear, our current process could never have evolved without the foundation laid by its predecessor; this is meant to be an illustrative example of our evolution and should encourage other organizations preparing to launch innovation capabilities to entertain beginning with a structure more resembling today's approach.

Commercialization Council

For an academic healthcare system, the initial gate where technologies are evaluated for viability and promise can take one of two forms: "an inch deep and a mile wide" or the inverse. The Commercialization Council was populated by motivated and knowledgeable physicians, scientists, and engineers from key areas of specialization who were known to be frequent contributors to the invention disclosure flow. Representation was broad, not necessarily deep, with one individual from each of several selected specialties.

Typically meeting bimonthly to quarterly, this body evaluated ideas using a standardized disclosure form, itself an early and important development and the predecessor of our present IDF. (See Appendix A.) The outcomes were binary, a thumbs-up or thumbs-down based upon collective wisdom and democratic process.

Imagine a single research scientist sitting next to an obstetrician, an ophthalmologist, and other specialists, and CCI asking them to opine on a specific implant modification that increases the longevity of total hip replacements. Even if the single representative from orthopaedic surgery was present, it was hard to convince an inventor we had the expertise around the table to make the best decision about his or her technology.

This lack of deep expertise, coupled with a somewhat subjective approach to ultimately determining feasibility, made the Commercialization Council effective, but not as efficient as we now have become. The shortcoming was not missing the next blockbuster—the council did an amazing job of picking the big winners. The limitation was a relative weakness in separating the solid and sustainable from the frail and failing. Furthermore, without a sophisticated instrument to do a deep dive into the technology, it was challenging to plot a path forward or even to look back with certainty on how or why specific decisions were made.

Everything in life falls onto a bell-shaped curve, so it's not surprising that the technologies that were one or two standard deviations from the mean in either direction got the appropriate attention and resources. The problem was that technologies under the middle of the curve tended to get too little attention to determine if they were champs or also-rans. The result was—you guessed it—delay and ambiguity.

Those twin curses were locked in a cause-and-effect relationship with the third inventor concern—lack of expertise of the evaluator. Again, this example is not meant to impugn the valued volunteers who populated our Commercialization Council, but to highlight the shortcomings of the initial filtering process. It is nearly impossible to expect even the most intelligent and engaged evaluator to know everything about each potential need or market.

Luckily, there were other forces at work that brought evolution to the PRCs: more interest and understanding of the innovation process and an increase in the number of disclosures from a more diversified field of inventors.

The Commercialization Council was pioneering and deserves respect—both the concept and the individuals who generously dedicated themselves to service. It was well suited for a nascent innovation function and provided the building blocks for CCI to become a worldwide leader in bringing ideas to the marketplace. Today, the stakes and inventor expectations are higher; the only constant is that resource allocation, including the time of experts to evaluate technology, remains challenging.

Peer Review Committees (PRCs)

You'll recall my two basic models of distributed expertise—"an inch deep and a mile wide" and the inverse. Our two decades of commercialization success, the velocity of medical innovation and the pressing need to transform healthcare have spawned a third model: "a mile deep and a mile wide."

Cleveland Clinic has the benefit of scale that germinated the concept of the PRC, with 3,200 physicians and scientists and more than 43,000 caregivers. We consider them all at the top of their game and potential innovators. Simultaneously, we have 400 to 500 invention disclosures per year from our campus alone. Both numbers increase when we include our Global Healthcare Innovations Alliance (GHIA) partners.[1]

With the anticipated quality and volume of disclosures generated in our environment, we required a strong mechanism to combat the trilogy of ambiguity. The answer was embodied in the PRCs.

After operating since the mid-1990s, the innovation and commercialization ecosystem at Cleveland Clinic had produced a large number of successful inventors, including those who enjoyed considerable financial return on their IP, either through a royalty-bearing license or equity in a spin-off company. Many were interested in giving back to the process that enriched them, as well as mentoring future generations of creators.

In addition, a fortuitous enterprise reorganization occurred in 2008. Cleveland Clinic is a vertically oriented, horizontally integrated multispecialty healthcare system. Our basic units of clinical care delivery departed from traditional academic departments and were reorganized around patient and pathology, becoming institutes. For example, orthopaedics and rheumatology were combined into the Orthopaedics & Rheumatology Institute. Neurology, neurosurgery, and psychiatry formed the Neurological Institute. The merits of this approach for the patients we serve are considerable. Aside from the convenience of physical colocation, the system or disease orientation promotes physician collaboration and efficiencies that translate into better care and patient experience.[2]

The direct benefit of the institute reorganization to the innovation process was that deep domain expertise was more easily solicited and accessed. We found that clinical and scientific leaders, many of whom had been successful innovators, were interested in deeper engagement in the commercialization process. We now had the logical assembly to evaluate technologies across the entire spectrum of care delivery with greater specificity and expertise.

Having multiple institute representatives populating the PRCs brought extraordinary breadth and depth of expertise to the front end of the evaluation process. For example, an orthopaedic disclosure is evaluated by five to eight fellow surgeons, usually all engaged inventors.

It became prestigious, in addition to fun and stimulating, to be involved in the PRCs. Institute leadership recognized the extra time demands, and we even saw a bump in the number of disclosures coming from PRC members.

So the final requirement was to equip the PRCs with an instrument that allowed them to objectively describe their thoughts on the current status of disclosed ideas and the potential of new innovations to transform their specialties. This was accomplished by developing multivariable technology scoring platforms. (See Figure 4.5.) Nine essential criteria were divided into three levels and weighted according to their influence on both practice and prospective adoption. Experts could score a disclosed technology from 1 to 5, depending on alignment with clearly articulated criteria.

The criteria are tough because the demands of investors and the marketplace are tough. The scorecard strips away wishful thinking from a proposal and helps to determine whether the idea is a superior one, can be built with existing technology, meets a demonstrable need, presents no extraordinary challenges, can be readily adopted by users, is based on verifiable principles, can compete for leadership in its space, and has a receptive target market.

The scorecard was a game changer because it directly addressed the exact concerns that our inventors were articulating all along. Now domain experts, usually inventors in their own right, were evaluating the intellectual contributions of their peers—just like refereed journals or grant applications.

One of the attractions of working at a great institution is the invisible power of culture that pervades every aspect of engagement. It comes back to that ubiquitous alignment with enterprise mission. We've never lacked for volunteers to populate and participate in our PRCs. The clinical and scientific leadership believe it is a duty and privilege to contribute to the innovation process in this fundamental manner.

With willing contributors and a steady flow of IP disclosures to assess, PRC meetings are held with regular frequency every four to six weeks. Inventors learn the fate of their technologies in a timely fashion and with objective evaluation criteria expressed across the multiple dimensions. While the inventor's clock is ticking continually during the development

FIGURE 4.5 Cleveland Clinic Innovations Scorecard. This represents original Peer Review Committee scorecard matrices. This process is dynamic and ever-evolving.

Criteria/Score	1	2	3	4	5
Improvement over Existing Practice	Inferior to existing technology	Some elements may be promising, but deficient compared to existing technology	Equivalent to existing technology	Moderate improvement over existing technology	Significant improvement over existing technology
Technical Feasibility	Technology requires extraordinary synergistic development to reach feasibility	Technology requires significant synergistic development to reach feasibility	Existing materials and "know-how" available for development & deployment with minimal difficulty and moderate costs	Existing materials and "know-how" available for development & deployment with modest incremental cost to institution	Technology can not only be readily developed, but may also provide a platform for further advances
Need Fulfillment	Fails to address established need	Partially addresses established need	Technology meets recognized clinical need	Technology potentially addresses new indications that have been identified or are being evaluated	Emerging indications identified and filled by technology
Commercialization Barrier (Risk Profile)	Extraordinary challenges perceived that would prevent or decelerate product development	Greater than average barriers to product development or specific domain impediments	Judged equivalent to historical product development barriers	Moderate development, regulatory, or adoption hurdles	Minimal development, regulatory, or adoption hurdles
Ease of Implementation	Technology must rely on considerable ancillary technology development and extensive caregiver education in order to reach implementation	Technology must rely on moderate ancillary technology development and extensive caregiver education in order to reach implementation	Ancillary technology/ "know-how" in place for successful implementation to AMCs and most secondary/tertiary care centers	Distributed expertise and technology to support implementation to majority of AMCs and other domestic practitioners	Widely accepted practices and readily available ancillary technology worldwide
Scientific/Regulatory Merit	Only "expert" opinion or clinical champion support exists	Modest representation in the scientific literature accompanied by uncontrolled studies	Similar technologies have been studied to level 3-4	Similar technologies have been studied to level 4	Similar technologies have been studied to level 5
Competitive/Market Advantage	Technology characteristics would be judged clearly inferior to existing, commercially available market	Technology characteristics would be judged acceptable but suboptimal to existing, commercially available market	Technology characteristics would be judged equivalent to existing, commercially available market	Technology characteristics would be judged moderately advantageous to existing, commercially available market	Technology characteristics would be judged clearly superior to existing, commercially available market
Likelihood of Peer Adoption	Characteristics of technology would impose considerable impediments to even modest adoption, disadvantageous cost/benefit analysis	Characteristics of technology would impose moderate impediments to adoption that would limit present and future adoption, likely costs fall outside value-basis	Objective & subjective criteria for practice adoption would likely be met for an average number of current practitioners, and may evolve with future practice, sensitivity to fiscal responsibility	Objective & subjective criteria for practice adoption would likely be met for a majority of current practitioners, neutral-to-advantageous value-basis	Strength of technology would change future practice patterns, resulting in widespread adoption and recognition as state-of-the-art, advantageous value-basis
Stage of Development	"Napkin Idea," rudimentary stage of ideation or proof-of-novelty	Modestly refined idea with sketches, preliminary prior art search, rudimentary modeling	Prior art search favorable, patient draft, prototype-ready, possible commercial awareness	Patent application, prototype-in-process, preliminary commercial interest	Patent granted, prototype produced and tested, identified commercial interest

cycle, the ticking is loudest and most anxiety-producing during the need assessment stage. When we became able to notify inventors within a specified time, their satisfaction skyrocketed.

Perhaps the most attractive component of the new PRC process was that inventors could react to an overall score as well as subcategory grades. This replaced the binary response that previously informed inventors only that their disclosure would either live or die, based upon a single show-of-hands vote. Even if the initial determination is that the technology needs improvement, there is an immediate and specific road map to enhance it. Precise deficiencies can be remedied more easily than vague objections.

Correspondingly, the scoring system has given CCI a mechanism by which we can validate our process and hone our capabilities. Initial scoring can now be corroborated by commercial success. We continually gain confidence regarding our adeptness at identifying winners and losers. This approach has improved our efficiency and resource deployment immeasurably.

We view the scoring system as a dynamic exercise. We are consistently evaluating the metrics that surround the process and its outcomes, and adjusting to take into account the market performance of the rated technologies. We believe that refreshing the methodology and membership of the PRCs will continue to be one of our key assets that differentiate our process.

NINE ESSENTIAL CRITERIA FOR EVALUATING INNOVATION DISCLOSURES

1. **Improvement over existing practice.** Is it better than what is already out there? Innovation for the sake of innovation, or making something different just for the intellectual exercise, is not the goal. The idea must deliver demonstrable advancement in the key criteria by which a developing technology will be judged.
2. **Technical feasibility.** Is it technically feasible? Can it be made? Will it work?
3. **Need fulfillment.** Does anyone need it? The innovation must be useful and desired by the target population.
4. **Commercialization barrier.** Are there any insuperable barriers to its development? It isn't just capital; most problems more money can solve aren't that big. Is there a barrier that cannot be overcome or navigated? Recognize the insurmountable and make the logical decision.
5. **Ease of implementation.** Can it be easily deployed? This speaks to scalability and transferability as much as the ability to produce the innovation. Is there an infrastructure to teach, monitor, and optimize use of an innovation outside the institution of origin? It is almost never too early to start thinking about how new technology will be disseminated and sustained.

6. **Scientific/regulatory merit.** Is it evidence-based? Regardless of the track record or status of the inventor, you must be as objective as possible. Look at the data. Respect the innovator, but don't permit blind faith or the cult of personality to dissuade you from seeking and trusting the real data.

7. **Competitive/market advantage.** Can it compete with the current leaders in its space? The goal is to exceed the existing technology in terms of quality, cost, efficiency, or outcome. Innovators may amplify their idea's defining characteristics and the margins of difference. There are many factors that contribute to ultimate success, but none more important than the fundamental innovation itself.

8. **Likelihood of peer adoption.** Is it likely to be adopted by the field? Pay attention to the differentiating elements of an innovation and how these could be communicated. They will be the handles that constituents will grasp, determining adoption. Subsequent performance and support in the marketplace will determine longevity and primacy.

9. **Stage of development.** Is it at an actionable stage of development for your organization? Practically no organization has unlimited resources, time, and money, so determine when to pass or partner.

Step 3: Determine the Innovation Destination: Commercialize, Monetize, Operationalize, Strategize

The role of an innovation unit in an organization's success is not confined to technology-transfer activities. Innovation leaders would agree that transformation in their enterprises will not occur simply by securing a few more patents or a handful of additional licenses. The reason to maintain a robust innovation function is to make the entire organization more innovative. The presence and influence of an innovation crucible can set the culture and stimulate both creative thinking and disciplined practice toward bringing new solutions to reality—regardless of whether they "spin in" or "spin off."

Innovation is a horizontal function, and it strengthens the fiber of most institutions that are, by nature, vertically organized into divisions, departments, or institutes. For this reason, innovation leaders must have an appreciation for both the overarching enterprise strategy and the aspirations of the individual organizational units. The way this plays out at Cleveland Clinic can best be understood by following the progression of new ideas through our process.

Once the PRC has opined, the nascent idea is considered an initially vetted and scored disclosure. Innovation functions must develop the antennae to determine whether an innovation has merit and to route the idea to its logical endpoint—or to say no or "not yet." Granted, not every creative disclosed IP results in a spin-off company or a royalty-bearing license. But that doesn't mean the remaining ones are not valuable, and we have emphasized a path for remediation and enhancement as a vital component of our process.

Although commercialization in the marketplace is the recognized outcome with which all are familiar, there are other ways to extract success and advance institutional goals with innovations that could deliver internal operational efficiencies or strategic advantage. The routing map for innovations emanating from a healthcare organization parallels that practiced in almost any business.

Ultimate decisions to spin off or spin in are complex; recognizing whether to direct innovations to the marketplace or retain them for strategic advantage is a critical skill that can be developed and measured. Admittedly, innovation on the campus of a healthcare system tends toward the model of disseminating scholarly research—we share our discoveries with the world. However, there are ideas that incrementally enhance processes or improve operational activities that may not have market traction but do create internal value.

To reiterate, the initial filter (CCI's PRCs, for example) should inform the innovator and the institution whether the disclosure has what it takes to undergo the journey to ultimate commercial utility. When scientific and technical merit are verified and clinical feasibility is validated, then something of value has been identified. The question that follows is how the greatest value can be extracted. There is not just one type or method of handling for creative thought. The potential outcomes usually considered by CCI include commercialize, monetize, operationalize, and strategize.

Commercialize

The most readily recognizable and concrete innovation outcome is traditional commercialization. In general, this is reserved for protectable (patent-worthy) IP, most of which resides in the medical devices and therapeutics and diagnostics domains. Licensing IP to a larger organization, resulting in a royalty-bearing license, or creating a spin-off company are familiar ways to capitalize on transcendent thought in these specific areas.

We employ the term *protectable IP* to highlight the difference between ideas that are patentable and those that are not. There are different types of patents. Utility patents reflect the technological novelty and process by which the mechanical or chemical entity works. In the United States, design patents are available that cover the ornamental appearance of an article. Design registrations may be secured abroad. There are additional mechanisms by which IP can be protected, including copyright, trademark, trade secrets, and international options, such as CE marking, which abbreviates *Conformité Européenne* and indicates compliance with all legislative requirements for European Union sale. Experienced IP attorneys are the best resource for directing the innovator toward the proper choice.

Verifying that there's no prior art, or evidence that the invention is not new, is often the first and fastest way to filter whether resources should be deployed for development. Innovators increasingly are performing their own preliminary patent searches on sources such as Google Patents. Most prolific creators have experienced the transient disappointment of learning that their "brand-new lightbulb" has been discovered by someone across the street or across the globe before they had the chance to announce it. The best do not wallow in defeat but go back to the drawing board.

If the professionals at CCI judge that the technology emerging favorably from our PRC process meets the criteria of novelty for a patent and would be served best by routing it to the commercial market through a license or company, then the next stop is one of our internal incubators. Modeled after the stand-alone incubator, which typically has more relevance after emerging companies are formed, our incubators are overseen by staff highly experienced in transactions with deep domain expertise.

Because of the large volume of disclosures and more mature IP that we manage, it's simply not feasible to build an operational, financial, and governance structure around each one. Instead, multiple evolving concepts can be managed via a portfolio approach until they reach the critical mass to attract the talent and capital necessary to get to the marketplace.

Our incubator leads are impressive—in many ways, it's harder to be the CEO of dozens of ideas than of a single company. Our leads continually bring their A game to please not a consolidated board of directors but individual inventors, themselves often acting as founders or CEOs.

Because these are homegrown technologies and processes, we don't have a competition for entry or a prescribed time for the development stage. Instead, the incubator is the perfect stop for an innovation after it's passed the technical filter and before market viability is determined by investment from outside entities.

Monetize

There is a difference between commercializing and monetizing. To commercialize involves the protection and transaction surrounding patented IP, while to monetize means to find new ways to leverage ideas and brand to create economic opportunity.

At Cleveland Clinic, we consider all of our colleagues to be experts, and there's value in the level of mastery each caregiver develops in his or her sphere. Can this expertise be converted into a salable article that extends beyond the walls of our institution? Can caregivers' know-how be defined, repackaged, and sold to others? The answer is often yes, and the intrinsic value is multiplied by brand identity and perceived level of achievement in the marketplace.

Cleveland Clinic is a $6.5 billion healthcare system. Forget for a minute that we exist to care for the sick, investigate their problems, and train future medical leaders. We manage large facilities, run a revenue cycle, direct a supply chain, operate parking facilities, serve thousands of meals, maintain a large fleet of vehicles, the list goes on. There is a great deal of expertise that accrues in the practice of these activities that can assist other hospital systems, as well as companies outside healthcare.

Caregivers engaged in these pursuits often see ways to improve incrementally how their jobs get done. Not infrequently, these caregivers also come up with disruptive advancements that may be industry-changing. This expression of innovation is just as valid as a new drug or device; these are transaction opportunities. In today's healthcare landscape, when value basis is the driver, advancements that improve access, elevate quality, and control cost are vital.

Do they need to be registered, and can they be protected? We leave that to the attorneys to decide. Many of the developments fall under copyright, trademark, or trade secret. This is especially true in the field of software development, where copyright law is catching up to the pace of innovation. Regardless of whether these innovations can be protected by traditional marks, they still can potentially be transacted.

A supplementary way an organization may capitalize on expertise is through an advisory or consulting function. For decades, organizations have turned to the large consulting houses for strategic direction and tactical improvements, but in recent years we've increasingly seen peer-to-peer information sharing. Possibly galvanized by the external pressures we all feel in healthcare, and inspired by the new sharing economy, there has been a paradigm shift in the competitor-collaborator relationship model.

Once an organization has conducted a seemingly simple, but absolutely vital introspection to determine "what makes us *us*," then core competencies can be codified and evaluated as teachable, scalable, or transferable. The plan to spin off the capability, and in what form, will eventually be a relevant discussion for the institutional and innovation leadership. So even if there's not a patent plaque to hang on the wall, there may be a check from an innovative monetization in the mailbox.

Operationalize and Strategize

These two potential outcomes are fundamentally different from the two preceding ones. Commercialization and monetization are basically spin-off results of the innovation process. They are outward-facing engagements that translate the innovation identity of an innovator or organization to the marketplace. They're designed to expand capability or brand awareness outside the walls of the organization in which they were gestated.

Two other innovation outcomes can be equally important, yet are not as readily identifiable. The difference resides in the predictors of their eventual success and influence on institutional practice.

The term *operationalize* describes the outcome for incremental process improvements that would be best developed and employed at the operational unit level. Ideas that may not have the qualities of protectable IP but could have substantive impact on patient care deserve to be treated as true innovations and also have the chance for their own impact trial. There are innumerable advancements that CCI never sees or that it immediately routes to the appropriate institute for further development and deployment. While plenty of these ideas undergo a similar litmus test to the one to which we subject marketable innovation, they are determined to be best developed and employed locally.

The *strategize* outcome is for innovations that may have institutional impact on competitive advantage. These are the "secret sauces" that create a margin of difference or distinguish a benefit in highly competitive markets. Institutional integration of innovation and strategic functions is required; innovation must not be marginalized from the overarching enterprise strategy, but instead interwoven with it. This is why so many individuals carry the dual title of "innovation and strategy officer"; these offices are physically and philosophically close.

What makes innovation-outcome decisions exciting yet challenging is the debate regarding whether to reveal and share versus integrate and operationalize. Would the idea garner more attention and potential revenue if commercialized? Or should the idea be developed within and then deployed to advance the enterprise? Obviously, such decisions are made case-by-case through discourse between the innovation hub and the C-suite.

It's the responsibility of the innovation officers to be the champions of the creator contributing ideas to be operationalized or strategized. Whatever the method by which recognition and reward is distributed at your enterprise, you must credit those individuals who supply creative energy and content that may not fall to the bottom line. Fullest investment in innovation creates a generous platform that can accommodate creative expression of all types, regardless of whether it can be patented or banked.

Step 4: Employ Internal Incubation and Advisory Services

The incubator stage is the pressure test for market viability following the clinical and technical validation of the PRC process. Instead of a veteran business builder stewarding a single entity, our internal incubators take a portfolio approach. Because the stage, size, and level of complexity of these aspiring companies or concepts lend themselves to an aggregated management strategy by an expert, we're able to advance multiple entities at a time. By leveraging shared services, internal and secured pools of proof-of-concept funds, and consistent contact with potential market acquirers, the incubator leader can successfully guide an ever-refreshing assembly of novel ideas.

Oversight provided by the incubator directors affords another unique advantage: they can detect complementary capabilities in two or more companies that may be fused into one in order to maximize success. This cross-pollination function could only be possible if one individual presides over the pool of emerging entities.

External advisory is also welcome at entry into the incubator and throughout the maturation of the progressing innovation. Early on, CCI recognized that the advice of experts in the investment and industrial sectors was vital for the success of mission-driven innovation. Inviting the marketplace in has been a key differentiator in our success. Establishing the Innovation Advisory Board has become a signature of our process and a model for others.

Unlike the PRC, the IAB provides the perspective of the marketplace, essentially presenting emerging technologies with the ultimate filter: will somebody buy or invest? Because the members are derived from the realms of venture capital, commercial innovation, institutional investment, corporate venture, and public policy, their viewpoints provide both immediate feedback and future direction for the most efficient and effective commercialization plans. Careful institutional policy analysis and development has created an environment in which direct investment by IAB members in the technologies they assess is permitted.

Interaction between the incubator directors and the IAB members is akin to a board of directors guiding the CEO of an early-stage company. Each interaction is a focused one that helps to determine the best plan for a technology's journey to the market. The difference lies in that incubator directors are managing a larger portfolio of companies in their respective domains. For this reason, IAB members are drawn from our "big four" (medical devices, therapeutics and diagnostics, HIT, and delivery solutions), but their diversified knowledge gained by investing across the spectrum makes their advice relevant to almost all technology and service innovations, at whatever stage.

I want to recognize the vital contribution of current and past members of the IAB to the development and present status of CCI. Our success has largely been predicated on activating and connecting all members of the innovation ecosystem. To a significant extent, the IAB is the capstone to our structure.

Step 5: Execute Transactions

In addition to the collective expertise I have described, we have a deal team. We're consistently negotiating with transaction pros from potential acquirers, so we must maintain competency.

Armed with fiduciary responsibility to optimally represent the inventor's technology, as well as the expectations of our institution, we've honed this craft over many years. Spinning off more than 70 companies and managing about 600 royalty-bearing licenses has afforded us domain-specific and market-relevant insight.

The flippant dismissal that "doctors aren't good at business" isn't an acceptable reality when you're charged with professionally managing the IP of your colleagues. We have approached business with medical ethics, but also with nothing less than a clear focus on achieving favorable outcomes for all parties involved in critical negotiations.

The backbone of our transactional arsenal is the finance committee of our Innovations Governance Advisory Board. Made up of our highest-level institutional officers, additional members of the office of the CFO, and selected members of the IAB, this ultimate connection with the enterprise ensures that we are making consistent and confident deals that align with our strategy and mission.

It's Not a Sport Until You Keep Score

Innovation is a discipline with measurable results that reflects and stimulates a creative culture. One of the catalysts allowing CCI to excel in mission-driven innovation is measurement of outcomes. Dashboard indicators of the inventive potential and production of our caregivers are tracked and analyzed monthly, including patent activity, invention disclosures, transaction activity, and accounting.

Initially, it may be exciting to recount anecdotal expressions of creativity at your institution, but it's not until you treat even the most innovative activity with objectivity that you join the modern practice of innovation. You must be able to plot your institution's performance metrics and compare your capabilities to those of leaders in your industry and others.

It's useful to monitor two broad sets of metrics: operational and outcome numbers. The former are barometers about how your process operates, and they illuminate pressure points that require attention if your institution's innovation group is to function at highest effectiveness. The latter define your innovation identity in the marketplace through commercial success and its downstream impacts.

Operational Metrics

Mission-driven innovation is essentially the *why* of our work, and throughout this book are best practices regarding *how* we've built a successful innovation engine. Operational metrics described *how well* we're doing our job.

Our innovation professionals are motivated to pursue constant improvement and innovate around their own processes to enhance output and satisfaction for inventors. They embrace that this as a dynamic process, and they must maintain flexibility. No two technologies are the same, as no two inventors are the same. We strive to have the fundamentals down, but we value being nimble enough to adjust on the fly.

The following are descriptions of some of the typical operational metrics we monitor and what they mean.

- **Number of disclosures.** The lifeblood of any innovation function is the flow of new ideas. The number of disclosures represents the turns "at bat" that an institution gets to develop meaningful IP. Maintaining an accessible yet detailed mechanism by which innovators can relate their novel concepts is critical, especially when it comes to patent protection. Our development of a web-based process for initial disclosure and tracking has been well received. To help increase the number of disclosures, we utilize all available internal communication channels to get the word out about our robust innovation entity. Our Inventors Forums bring creative minds together and disseminate information to a large group simultaneously.

- **Number of returned/advanced disclosures.** If the raw number of disclosures represents the "at bats," then the disposition of these into the incubator stage, reflecting viable ideas from a clinical or technical standpoint, provides the numerator for calculating the "batting average." When mature, an organization may experience an increase in both the number of disclosures and their quality, but in the beginning, the best way to improve batting average is to conduct a thorough analysis of the technology by domain experts at the outset.

■ **Number of patent applications.** Patents aren't the only route to recognize intellectual accomplishment, but patents *are* the acknowledged vehicle for protecting IP. One decision that may face the sophisticated innovation leader is in what geographies to protect IP. For that discussion, it's best to include the innovator who knows international practice patterns and a seasoned patent attorney with strong global experience.

■ **Amount of time between submission and decision.** Keeping score shouldn't simply be confined to volume or dollars. One of the most sensitive indicators of the performance of a commercialization engine is its timing in hitting milestones. This is especially true because inventors are appropriately impatient; they want to know the fate of their ideas, and this is true for the initial step and for subsequent steps as well. To enhance communication, as well as to hone our own processes, we've instituted electronic databases that track the progress of the disclosure through every step of our INVENT process. The inventor can monitor the progress, and just as important, the innovation managers can identify bottlenecks or underperforming assets.

■ **Number of resubmitted disclosures.** Most people don't think of this one. However, if your evaluation process is fully developed, a remediation plan should accompany all but the IP nullified by prior art. This demonstrates the value of having multiple dimensions for evaluating technologies and ways to specifically describe the pluses and minuses of an inventor's submission. If the process is executed correctly, the inventor will not only have the opportunity to resubmit an initially declined technology, but will have a road map regarding how to pursue improvement. Don't just discard ideas that didn't make the first cut; have a remediation function that follows a prescribed plan. We encourage the innovator to contemplate, refine, and resubmit the idea. You'd be surprised how some reflection and direction can resurrect an embryonic idea and ultimately get it over the finish line if the inventor is not discouraged but mentored.

- **Inventor satisfaction.** Dollars and cents are important, but the innovation function can never lose sight of the fact that it's a service organization. Develop objective and subjective systems to ask inventors for feedback on how you're doing. Open discourse about performance sharpens your capabilities and creates an even greater connection. Comfort and trust are critical lubricants to what can be an arduous process; these are best maintained by consistent communication and adherence to a service mentality. There is a fundamental difference between *criticism* and *critical analysis*; request the latter from your inventors, and use the information constructively when addressing your colleagues' work.

There are publicly reported numbers often used as benchmarks for institutional performance, such as those from the Association of University Technology Managers. I believe that engaging in comparison between institutions or in some form of ranking is largely unproductive. This may sound contrarian for one who espouses objectivity in analyzing the performance of his unit, but there's not a lot of logic in scoring innovation production against the yardstick of another institution.

Innovation is not a competitive race between organizations. The factors that contribute to the number of disclosed or patented technologies or the number of spin-off companies can be fairly opaque. The value in recording metrics over time resides in determining the trajectory of your own group, year-on-year. If done with intellectual honesty and a dash of intuition, the answers that emerge from keeping an eye on trends can be invaluable.

An "innovation quotient," or a level of IP flow, will eventually reveal itself as an innate characteristic. The reason why our practice may never come up with a true "IQ" is that the denominator is elusive. It's exceedingly difficult to determine the divisor in the innovation equation—is it number of caregivers, size of technology transfer operation, research dollars, etc.? You get the idea. It's possible to identify the number of patents or the size of the transaction, but nearly impossible to pick the right denominator.

This is why we usually tell organizations that the denominator is best considered *your institution*, until we can determine a better way to measure the variables. Your organization, assuming stability of size and dedication to a sustained business focus, will exhibit an inevitable leveling off in number of disclosures. It is then that you can determine how to rightsize your innovation apparatus and adjust the expectations of leadership around measurable outcomes.

Outcome Metrics

Sometimes we use the term *outcome* when we're really speaking about *income*. That is partially true here, but tracking innovation success goes beyond the monetary measure. It's frustrating that we can never really track the most important result of our ideas and the labors directed to bringing them into practice, the impact on the patient. As a substitute, we follow numbers that are relevant to our function.

- **Number of granted patents.** Many variables affect the ultimate procurement of a U.S. patent. It's an achievement that turns an innovator into an inventor, and it should be a source of great pride and accomplishment. Innovation leaders should not only keep track of granted patents, they should celebrate them. We give the inventor a plaque with the first page of the patent emblazoned and recognize inventors at an inventors' annual dinner. It's a big deal to have a creative thought turn into a tangible advancement that will be forever memorialized. Celebrate it!

- **Royalty-bearing licensing activity.** Somewhere along the way, a decision becomes evident regarding the dispensation of a particular technology or suite of IP. Should it be licensed or spun off? A minority can stand alone and develop into a spin-off company, while a decided majority are attractive to larger operating entities to enhance their catalogs; such transactions are licenses. I've been disappointed that there is an outsize focus on spinning off companies, while royalty-bearing licenses are relegated to the backseat. We educate our inventors about the value of licensing technology and the recurring financial benefits they can receive. As seductive as it may sound to get the six- or seven-figure payday that may be associated with a company acquisition based on your technology, the veritable "home run," hitting a bunch of singles and doubles isn't a bad strategy. Our experience is that education, expectation setting, and common sense are valuable tools when discussing dispensation of technology with all institutional stakeholders. Don't try to force every development into a mold for which it may not be best suited.

- **Number and valuation of spin-off companies.** I've already lamented that our innovations community has become entranced by quantity over quality when it comes to spin-off companies. Hanging another logo in your reception area can be a badge of honor in the game of moving a large number of ideas down the path of commercialization. But there are two cautions to avoid: (1) overly incentivizing your innovation leaders to produce spin-offs, and (2) demoting the opportunity for a lucrative license and holding out too long because a spin-off is "sexier." Go in with an open mind, and let the educated discussion of stakeholders and the market dictate the right choice.

This scorecard of operational and outcome metrics forms a solid basis for launching or refreshing an institutional innovation function. Tracking these parameters lets you know *your* game. Innovation is not a pursuit in which benchmarking is either logical or healthy; perhaps you can pressure a physician to see three more patients per clinic to increase her numbers, but you can't extract more innovation from a creative mind by waving benchmark data in the face of an inventor. Likewise, if the hospital system across town or the university across the country has more patents or licensing revenue than yours, it didn't use up the "creative karma" in the universe and leave you inadequately resourced to come up with the next idea. It's not a zero-sum game.

Work on optimizing your own innovation process, and the results will follow—some dollars, some handshakes, and many patient lives improved or extended.

It's Not the Big That Eat the Small— It's the Fast That Eat the Slow

A final variable remains: the elusive and ubiquitous influence that Father Time has on everything we do in innovation.

When the prize is a first-to-market or first-mover advantage, then speed matters. The challenges to innovation, especially in academic settings, can range from institutional inertia and lack of infrastructure to the arduous patent process and regulatory hurdles. Acceleration in innovation is not achieved by cutting corners, but by learning efficiencies, economy of action, and the power of simultaneous versus sequential action. Identifying choke points and developing strategies to alleviate them is the purview of the chief innovation officer.

Another way time impacts the innovation process concerns the decisions regarding when and how to pull the plug on a technology. Innovation leaders often speak of the Three Fs of successful innovation: fast, frugal failure. The innovation champion must learn how to filter the promising solutions from the inferior ones. It's always tough to sundown a project, but the anguish is multiplied when you've nurtured and resourced it, or worse yet, practiced alongside its originator.

At CCI, we've equipped ourselves with the right tools so we won't be the limiting factor. We've also identified appropriate milestones and processes common to the development of most technologies in key domains.

Some ideas die natural deaths, while others linger before the determination that they were ahead of their time or market demand, didn't have ultimate customer appeal, or would consume too many resources or too much effort per unit. I'd simply remind innovation leaders to keep an eye on the clock, while also looking at the dashboards constructed from the elements discussed previously. There's a reason why some projects take longer, but when the calendar drags out of proportion to your experience and the market cycle, the initiative itself may be begging to be put out of its misery.

The most successful organizations are intrinsically agile—nimble in delivery by seizing advantage of opportunity windows. This means having sufficient resources to direct to the "next big thing" when necessary. If your resources are deployed in life support for failing concepts, you'll never realize the benefits of speed.

The business of innovation has been portrayed alternatively as a marathon or a sprint. Nowadays, it feels like a marathon at sprinter's pace. Unpromising projects shackling your ankles will prevent you from reaching the finish line in a timely manner to satisfy inventors or conserve your resources. The answer is to build time sensitivity into all of your processes and honor it just as much as dollars, patents, and spin-off companies.

Products

Completing the Virtuous Cycle

The ultimate goal of mission-driven innovation is the improvement and extension of human life. There is a genuine idealism at the core of our work. Yet some people blame the rising cost of medical technology for the nation's current crisis in healthcare costs, which is not a fair accusation. In fact, the contrary is true. The virtuous cycle of medical innovation actually helps to control the cost of healthcare delivery. To help make this case, I'm going to describe the products of the virtuous cycle. I'll break them down into four principle domains and review some of the obstacles that must be overcome before products find their way to patients' bedsides. I'll make the case that medical innovation is a worthwhile pursuit from an economic standpoint. Finally, I'll introduce a process that is in many ways the social counterpart to mission-driven innovation: value-based innovation.

Outputs and Outcomes

To evaluate medical innovation in general, we have to understand its outputs in particular. For many in healthcare, medical innovation means hardware: surgical instruments, prosthetics, and imaging devices. But it also includes pharmaceuticals and, increasingly, software. At Cleveland Clinic Innovations (CCI), we divide our innovation activities into four domains, each corresponding to a distinct output. They are:

- Medical devices

- Therapeutics and diagnostics (Pharma)

- Health information technology (HIT)

- Delivery solutions

Let's look at each domain, review its products, and consider some factors that may influence the cost of bringing them to market.

Medical Devices

Medical hardware has historically dominated CCI's portfolio of gestating devices. Although it makes up 60 percent today, it was as high as 66 percent in 2008. This is typical of any innovation function in its early years. It's easier to organize your efforts around something everyone can see, understand, and touch.

This emphasis on tangible devices in part reflects Cleveland Clinic's long history of device innovation. Since the 1920s, our clinicians have continually improved the tools of the trade, from surgical retractors to gastroscopes. The other reason CCI rose to prominence as a commercialization engine for medical devices is rooted in the industrial heritage of the region and the "maker's spirit" that pervades local culture.

CCI was founded in this spirit. To grow a world-class medical device commercialization function, we needed to aggregate, maintain, and refine our model-building, legal, and regulatory capabilities. We recruited biomedical engineers and built them a sophisticated fabrication shop with five-axis milling machines, 3-D printers, lathes, and experts to run them. We assembled a legal team with experience in the protection of intellectual property (IP) in the device space and regulatory expertise to help navigate the U.S. Food and Drug Administration (FDA) environment.

Our labs brought forth one solid, weighable object after another: artificial hips, hearts, and kidneys; valves, clips, and instrumentation; stents to keep vessels open; and patches to keep wounds closed.

Our orientation toward device development has reflected national industrial trends. Medical devices play a significant role in the U.S. economy. About three-quarters of the medical device companies with annual revenues of over $1 billion are based in the United States. Medical devices are one of the few sectors that are consistently net exporters. In fact, exports of medical devices nearly doubled in the decade between 1998 and 2008 to more than $33 billion annually.

But past performance does not equal future success. Several factors challenge U.S. dominance of the medical innovation field.

The most prominent is the 2.3 percent excise tax on U.S.-made or imported medical devices legislated under the Affordable Care Act. The effect of this tax has been hotly debated. Manufacturers consider it a burden and job killer, warning that its adoption will move as much as 10 percent of device manufacturing offshore, accompanied by a loss of 43,000 jobs.[1] No one will be spared its negative effects, not the smallest shop nor the largest strategic company. Many believe this tax is inherently biased against emerging entrepreneurial concerns.

Advocates of the tax, including nonpartisan research groups like the Center on Budget and Policy Priorities, dismiss detractors' facts as distortions and foresee little effect on medical device innovation.[2] They maintain that repealing the tax would cost $26 billion over the period 2015–2024.[3] Whichever side is right, the scale and vehemence of the debate contributes to the atmosphere of uncertainty in the innovation field.

In addition to taxes, the federal government also imposes a lengthy process to gain approval from its principal regulator, the FDA, which often is criticized for being slow, being inconsistent, and lacking transparency.

Innovation players in the United States, including CCI, often work around the FDA by taking advantage of the European Union's (EU) more timely approval process. Many rollout plans begin by seeking CE (*Conformité Européenne*) marking, which permits the sale of products in the EU. Although it is not the equivalent of FDA approval, CE marking allows you to get your product out into a marketplace somewhere and provides useful data for everyone involved.

Other potential checks on innovation include ongoing uncertainty about the future of the U.S. research and experimentation (R&E) tax credit, a provision meant to promote innovation by making research activities less expensive for business. Currently, the research tax credit is being extended only by one-year increments. No one can say from year to year how long it will last, and this uncertainty deters investment. Some believe that the tenuous future of the tax credit is discouraging scientists and physician-innovators overseas from bringing their talents to America.[4]

Fortunately, innovators don't turn their brains on or off in response to legislative or regulatory vicissitudes. CCI remains optimistic about device development. There is tremendous scope to do good in the device sector, and I continue to recommend it as the best starting place for a young and growing mission-driven innovation function.

Therapeutics and Diagnostics

Pharmaceuticals are sometimes called *molecules* for short. But there is nothing short about the FDA approval process for these compounds. It is long and arduous and can go on for more than a decade.

The multistep process of drug discovery has many specialized components, from medicinal chemistry to regulatory navigation. It is also one of the costliest journeys in all of medical innovation. The price tag of bringing a new drug to market often nears or exceeds $1 billion. This factors in a high failure rate: for every 5,000 to 10,000 compounds entering the research and development pipeline, only one emerges with FDA approval.

So why engage in an endeavor that sends so many bright technical minds chasing projects that statistically fail far more often than they succeed, while soaking up huge budgets? Because a single success can assuage the suffering of millions of patients and produce an economic windfall that can offset any number of expensive failures.

Today we are seeing more optimism about drug discovery than ever before. Science and medicine are beginning to understand human disease on a molecular level with more clarity. Terms such as the *Human Genome Project, precision medicine,* and *designer drugs* are familiar to everybody, and the innovation world is gearing up to apply these data to target therapies.

Drug development proceeds according to a series of predictable stages. Each stage adds complexity and expense to the process. Here is a rundown of the journey from ideation to approval. (See Appendix B for a detailed description of each stage.)

- Organic research

- Target identification and validation

- Determination of a "lead compound"

- ADME/tox testing

- Compound optimization

- Preclinical testing

- Investigational New Drug (IND) Application

- Clinical trials (Phases 1, 2, and 3)

- New Drug Application (NDA)

- Manufacture and scaling

- Phase 4 testing

Innovators who contribute the next blockbuster drug that lowers cholesterol or controls diabetes not only must be intelligent and creative, they must have extraordinary perseverance. There may be no other domain in innovation that is more challenging to navigate and riskier to engage in.

Success in the pharmaceutical industry can be extremely lucrative. The overall value of the global pharma market is over $300 billion per year. This figure is projected to top $400 billion in the next three to five years. The 10 largest pharmaceutical firms control a quarter to a third of the market, and each has sales in the neighborhood of or exceeding $10 billion and profit margins approaching 30 percent. Of course, there are those who argue that business goals and the pursuit of profit are at cross-purposes with public health concerns; these are legitimate debates that are beyond the scope of this book. But one thing is certain: it takes a great deal of investment in the overall process to find the "needle in the haystack" that becomes a commercially viable drug.

Today, therapeutics and diagnostics accounts for 17 percent of CCI's IP portfolio. From the perspective of an academically based innovation engine, drug discovery is one of the most difficult endeavors to go alone. While medical devices and HIT development can comfortably reside on our campuses, it usually requires an industrial partner for the journey from bench to bedside when trying to bring a new drug to the market. The CCI strategy has been to identify valued partners with interests in specific disease states or families of compounds and develop lasting relationships that lead to more efficient transit through the multiyear gestation of a new compound. Having a partner to navigate the technical, economic, and regulatory hurdles is almost imperative if one is to be successful in this area.

For example, Cleveland Clinic is among several investors in the privately held regenerative medicine company Juventas Therapeutics Inc., whose primary product is a stromal cell–derived factor that protects and repairs damage to organ tissue resulting from a broad range of pathologic insults. The company's nonviral gene therapies have demonstrated meaningful results in human studies for the treatment of chronic heart failure and late-stage peripheral artery disease.

Our association with the Lubrizol Corporation through the Global Healthcare Innovations Alliance (GHIA) brings an in-depth understanding of polymer chemistry and specific expertise in drug delivery solutions. Lubrizol's 2014 acquisition of Vesta, a leading medical device contract manufacturer, enhances our collaboration via advanced capability in thermoplastic extrusion and silicone fabrication, elements that will directly benefit drug delivery strategies.

It's fortunate that those contributors of new therapies aren't easily daunted by long odds and multiple hurdles. Whether it is the occasional anti-inflammatory you take after a sports injury or a lifesaving chemotherapy, new drugs are one of the greatest gifts of medical innovation.

Health Information Technology

HIT is the most potent driver of healthcare transformation today. In contrast to the length and expense of the pharmaceutical cycle, HIT can be developed and deployed rapidly.

Cleveland Clinic was among the first to embrace the electronic medical record (EMR) in 2002. Since then, we have built a comprehensive system that connects our more than 90 care delivery sites across the United States and the Middle East. But HIT is more than electronic medical recordkeeping. It includes the use of patient data for research and planning purposes, distance health applications, e-prescribing, storage and transfer of personalized health records, health information exchange, and network intra-operability. These functions are an essential part of virtually every plan for cost control and healthcare reform.

According to McKinsey & Co.'s 2011 Global Institute report, *Big Data: The Next Frontier for Innovation, Competition, and Productivity,* "If U.S. healthcare were to use big data creatively and effectively to drive efficiency and quality, the sector could create more than $300 billion in value every year. Two-thirds of that would be in the form of reducing U.S. healthcare expenditures by about 8 percent."[5]

Big data has been responsible for many of our early successes in HIT innovation. But the current vanguard is making the EMR more interactive with patients and caregivers and distributing it across a variety of platforms. Cleveland Clinic innovators have developed or adopted dozens of mobile apps to help them educate patients and better understand and diagnose disease, and many more are in the works.

One example is the Cleveland Clinic Concussion (C3) app developed by Jay Alberts of our Neurological Institute. The app utilizes the iPad's gyroscope and accelerometer to collect biomechanical data that are used objectively to quantify postural stability while an individual performs balance tests with the iPad secured at the waist. The C3 app also assesses cognitive function through tasks performed with a stylus on the iPad screen. The app is being utilized by high school and college sports teams across the nation for baseline testing and deployment by athletic trainers, physicians, and physical therapists across the injury spectrum. Refinements are under way to evaluate mild traumatic brain injury in military personnel and assess deep brain stimulation in patients with Parkinson's disease.

Another example is a new video visits app for Ohio residents, MyCare Online, which offers patients 24-hour access to a medical professional for urgent care needs. The app connects patients with a healthcare provider via iOS or Android devices. Providers can assess, diagnose, and treat patients' conditions as well as prescribe medication. MyCare Online's service costs $49 per visit, which patients pay for with a credit card directly on the app.

As an innovation and commercialization function, CCI is trying to determine the best practice to protect and advance the solutions coming from our entire health system and global alliance. We do this by continually refreshing our understanding of the caregiver-patient relationship, specifically, where and how it takes place, what data is generated when they are connected, and how the information guides the patient's next steps toward better health. This is not a change in the fundamental belief that the center of the medical universe is where the caregiver and patient come together; it is recognition that it may not happen in the traditional way because of information technology advancement.

With this in mind, we strive to "touch all the bases" that appear to be the most important for success in HIT development. Here is our checklist of questions:

- Can we affect access to care, quality of outcome, and healthcare cost by optimizing the way technology, providers, and patients interact?

- Can we create solutions that help patients and caregivers to connect and exchange information through mobile devices and online?

- Can we provide actionable data that allows patients to personalize their healthcare experience and assists them in navigating the medical system?

- Can we develop and maintain conduits for exchange of private healthcare information (both care-related and transactional) that require the highest level of security?

- Can we deliver the most current, evidenced-based information to caregivers at the point of contact to facilitate decisions that help patients?

HIT was once considered a discipline that was distant from the core of an innovation function because it wasn't implanted (medical devices) or ingested (therapeutics and diagnostics). Today, managing HIT disclosures has become a centerpiece of our activity and nearly a quarter of our IP portfolio, just as the impact of advanced data management has become one of the most important determiners of the future of healthcare.

Delivery Solutions

What makes Cleveland Clinic, Cleveland Clinic? Of course, it's the caregivers living our mission on behalf of patients. But what intellectual contributions create the distinguishing characteristics that deliver the margin of difference that truly defines us? Not simply the definable, episodic disclosures that are routed into one of the three domains described previously, but the processes and approaches that affect the day-to-day delivery of care?

A more pertinent question for an innovation leader is to ascertain whether those nuggets of information or organic practices can be captured and monetized. At the intersection of innovation and strategy resides the domain incubator we call delivery solutions. Management of IP in this domain brings unique challenges and opportunities that sometimes find their way to an institutional innovation function; being prepared to develop or route them appropriately can determine their success and impact.

I have purposely avoided the term *consulting* because I don't want to confuse that discipline with building the infrastructure and practice of developing distinct IP that we consider "innovation." However, it's in the handling of core competencies and "packaging" them for consumers outside their point of origin that the lines blur. Furthermore, there's the possibility that a unique strength could offer such a strategic advantage that it will be handled better as a "spin-in" and deliberately withheld from outside distribution, even if it could be commercialized.

These are the "secret sauces" that may increase efficiency, improve outcomes, or control costs. We have experienced that other medical systems want to know how we administer everything from our supply chain to our revenue cycle, even our innovation function. The advice I would give stewards of the innovation function is that they need to be prepared to field ideas from all parts of their organizations and be intimately familiar with how these should be guided according to institutional directive. Perhaps the best mechanism is to have a triage point where these ideas can be channeled. Bringing a disciplined approach to the evaluation and triage of ideas is the essence of innovation. While some may be shiny metal objects, pills, or lines of code that are tangible and easily directed, others are just good ideas. Maintaining a methodology to route these appropriately, whether spun off or spun in, may provide the margin of difference across all innovation domains.

HYBRIDS

If organic innovation is stimulated optimally at the intersection of disparate knowledge sets, then it would logically follow that combining ideas from two or more of the innovation domains described could create even more potent advances. Here are two examples of how Cleveland Clinic's brilliant inventors and CCI's innovation infrastructure brought to life ideas from adjacent sectors that resulted in advances that were greater than the sum of their parts.

Combining Medical Devices and Therapeutics and Diagnostics: Infuseon Therapeutics, Inc.

A consistent challenge encountered in treating aggressive brain tumors is how to achieve the necessary concentrations of chemotherapeutic agents into the tumor. Even if some medications have been shown to be effective, how can they be safely administered, given that the chemical watchdog of the brain, the semipermeable blood-brain barrier, may not allow selected molecules to cross?

Talented Cleveland Clinic neurosurgeon Michael A. Vogelbaum and colleagues at our GHIA partner Parker Hannifin Corp. developed a new multiport catheter technology for drug delivery directly into brain tumors. The Cleveland Multiport Catheter™ is protected by two U.S. patents and is the basis for a spin-off company, Infuseon Therapeutics, Inc.

The catheter has already been deployed in patients with considerable success, while intense study of its results for the FDA is ongoing. The device that Dr. Vogelbaum developed is groundbreaking, but what it invites is an entirely new direction in drug development—chemotherapeutic agents that can be delivered through the new device directly into the tumor.

Now medicinal chemists and drug researchers can turn their attention to identifying molecules, adjusting concentrations, and evaluating protocols that can be used in a completely different way. The result will likely be a new family of direct chemotherapeutic agents that will be distinguished for both their route of delivery and their efficacy for some of the most devastating brain tumors afflicting patients.

Combining Medical Devices and Health Information Technology: Custom Orthopaedic Solutions, Inc.

One of the greatest breakthroughs to improve quality of life and relieve suffering for those afflicted with bone and joint problems has been the advent of artificial joints. Total hips, knees, shoulders, elbows, and the like are becoming so commonplace that there are few who haven't had the procedure or don't know someone who has.

One of the major concerns with the replacement of a native joint with a synthetic one is the wear characteristics: metal and plastic just aren't as durable as our own bone and cartilage. The rate at which the artificial joint wears ultimately determines its longevity. Although 10 to 20 years is a possible life span of a total joint arthroplasty, extending this interval for procedures that are done hundreds of thousands of times a year has obvious merit. It has also been determined that almost one-third of total joint revisions are due to inaccurate or imprecise intraoperative implant positioning.

HYBRIDS, *continued*

One of the ways orthopaedic surgeons and engineers improve the durability of implants is to make them more "anatomic." They can choose materials that are more biocompatible, but it is the fundamental design that likely affects the performance more than any other preoperative factor. The other variable in the equation is what happens in the operating room, when the surgeon actually implants the joint. Even nearly perfect implants can yield inferior results when placed at incorrect angles or rotations.

Founded in 2011 by orthopaedic surgeons Wael K. Barsoum and Joseph P. Iannotti, with help from software engineer Jason A. Bryan, Custom Orthopaedic Solutions, Inc. (COS) designs, develops, and manufactures products that improve surgical accuracy, leading to better patient outcomes. Using a combination of sophisticated computer programs and equally advanced fabrication tools, COS produces refined surgical planning tools, patient-specific bone models, and intelligent surgical instruments all focused on providing the surgeon with the best tools to tackle complex cases.

The by-product of better planning and enhanced three-dimensional understanding of the anatomy is greater surgical efficiency and fewer complications. Translation: higher-quality outcomes for patients and increased value to hospitals or health systems.

COS not only inhabits but has pioneered the intersection of where the computer meets the 3-D printer, and their progeny is a road map for surgeons and provides tangible models for them to manipulate. All of these factors collaborate to make doctors better and patients healthier for longer periods.

The Value of Medical Innovation

U.S. healthcare spending has been growing by almost 10 percent a year since 1970; its share of the economy has doubled over those years; and per capita spending for healthcare nearly doubled in the decade and a half between 2001 and 2015 (2001: $5,168; 2015: $9,146).[6] The ultimate payer for almost 60 percent of the cost of healthcare is government.

Everyone involved in healthcare understands that these high costs are not sustainable. As a result, both the government and private payers are moving the industry toward a new payment model. The old model was volume-driven, episodic, and expensive. The new model is value-driven, with value defined as change in clinical outcome divided by cost of care. If medicine is moving to a value basis, so should innovation. As a pioneer in mission-driven innovation, CCI is doing its part to open the next chapter in commercialization and corporate venturing, value-based innovation.

Value-based innovation can be defined as delivering solutions for big problems affecting large populations more quickly, more efficiently, and less expensively.

One of the primary goals of describing the true character of the mission-driven innovation ecosystem is to solicit all stakeholders to engage in practices that balance the objectives of each respective participant with the overall purpose of the current healthcare landscape. If all players are informed of the definition of value-based innovation, then the collective power will be directed to this worthy pursuit.

There is probably no transaction in the history of commerce in which both participants did not want to ensure that they got a good deal. There is also likely no other value equation that is harder to calculate and more difficult to defend than that of engaging in the endeavor of medical innovation. That is because the cost of innovation can be tracked, but its net effect is practically incalculable.

Many innovation leaders have spent their careers trying to correct the misperception that innovation is expensive, that it simply adds expense to the medical system. For example, the cost of developing penicillin can be tallied, but how do you calculate the benefit of restoring health?

The philosophical dispute is difficult to win, especially with the myopic persons who refuse to take into account the intangible, let alone the tangible, benefits of medical innovation. Fortunately, more scholarly research is being done to promote the position that medical innovation is a sound investment in the health and wealth of our country. Here are a few arrows for the quiver of the innovation champion when next locked in debate about the value of medical innovation:

- What happened to diseases like smallpox and polio, even death from heart attack or HIV/AIDS? Medical advancement has eradicated or significantly altered the course of these scourges.

- The National Bureau of Economic Research (NBER) reported that between 1960 and 1997, new therapies accounted for 45 percent of the increased life expectancy in 30 developing and high-income countries; between 2000 and 2009, new therapies were credited with increasing life expectancy by 73 percent.[7]

- The NBER paper also revealed that for every dollar spent on innovative medicines, total healthcare spending is reduced by $7.20.[8]

- In 2006, the *Journal of Political Economy* estimated that over the preceding 50 years medical innovation had been the source of nearly half of the economic growth in the United States.[9]

- A 2007 Milken Institute paper reported that cancer treatment results in a tenfold increase in occupational productivity, specifically $37 billion of cancer treatments resulted in an estimated $373 billion in economic productivity in treated cancer patients.[10]

- In the vernacular of Ehrlich and Becker, therapeutic and prophylactic medical technologies serve as "self-insurance" and "self-protection" that diminish the impact of illness and disease or decrease its probability respectively.[11] Experts can calculate the so-called insurance value of medical innovation and estimate that the total insurance value of creative, commercialized advancements adds 166 percent to their traditional valuations and that the total insurance value of technology is approximately seven times the total value of health insurance itself.[12]

Unlike in the typical vendor-client or producer-consumer relationship, the recipient of the ultimate product in a medical transaction often doesn't want it (patients wouldn't choose to be sick or injured), and they often don't pay for it, at least directly, as third-party payers intervene in that exchange. Maybe this is why the true cost-benefit relationship of technology development has been so evasive.

We shouldn't be completely blind to the fiscal repercussions of operating the most productive and expensive innovation crucible in the world. However, we should be prepared to balance the uninformed claims of critics who see technology development only as a driver of healthcare expenditure and not as a provider of productivity and prosperity.

Value-based innovation will deliver devices and drugs of less expense but equal or greater efficacy and technologies and techniques that make processes more efficient. Every stakeholder believes that it's time for this paradigm shift.

Value-based innovation can be integrated into the very fiber of the innovation process by guiding our talented innovators to look critically at the big problems and integrate cost consciousness into their creative process. We can educate inventors and investors about the margin of difference created by value and adjust the filters used to winnow the inventions portfolio. Innovative thought will gravitate toward advancements that meet the value criteria, and investment dollars will follow.

In closing, I must clarify two issues. I don't eschew the needs of so-called "orphan diseases"; I anticipate continued commitment from academic medicine and industry to select problems suffered by only a few patients—it's the right thing to do. Second, I believe key players will collaborate to solve the most pressing big problems, even when considerable resources are required.

The product of innovation viewed from the outside is a new implant, drug, software program, or process. The product of medical innovation for those of us who live it every day is the improved health of a single patient, an entire community, a country—and the whole world.

Practices

Are You Ready to Lead Innovation?

Just like a purposeful device or an elegant molecule, the practice of innovation has a structure and function that determine its level of success. This chapter will detail how diverse types of innovation, contributing a variety of solutions, move through an institution's innovation infrastructure. We'll also cover the basic proprietary tools that Cleveland Clinic Innovations (CCI) has developed to assess the value of individual technology disclosures and the preparedness of entire institutions to participate in structured innovation.

At its core, successful innovation is about execution. While CCI's success is due to identifying promising technologies, it is equally derived from appropriately saying no and shutting down projects to suitably direct time and resources.

While exercising discipline in the handling of disclosed technologies may be paramount, almost as critical is developing an understanding of the various mechanisms by which mission-driven innovation is derived. Experience and insight is required to recognize and gestate ideas emanating from the different routes by which innovation is fostered. Expertise in both the intake and development processes maximizes the chances of success. Ultimately, this level of mastery allows the institutional innovation practice to be sustainable and scalable.

The Six Degrees of Innovation

In CCI's nearly two decades of experience, we've identified six distinct varieties of innovation. In cataloging them, I've been inspired by Peter Drucker, who has contributed many concepts germane to our understanding of innovation and entrepreneurship.

There's elegance in the simplicity by which he communicates the seven sources of innovation in his landmark book, *Innovation and Entrepreneurship: Practice and Principles*.[1] This fundamental work inspired us to think more deeply about the varieties of mission-driven innovation, and we came up with a slightly different, yet intersecting approach called *six degrees of innovation*.[2] We chose the term *degrees* to reflect the degrees of a compass. A compass is a fitting metaphor, as a sense of direction, along with organizational nimbleness, to adjust to changing conditions is crucial to the accomplished innovator. Additionally, a compass is an instrument that tracks where you have been and beckons you to unexplored territory on the journey—in this case, to cover the entire innovation landscape.

First-Degree Innovation: Opportunistic

F. Mason Sones, Jr., after whom the annual award recognizing Cleveland Clinic's top innovator is named, was regarded personally as a curmudgeon, professionally as a genius. Though his seminal discovery of coronary angiography was made in 1958, his name is still invoked with just deference for the innovation's huge impact on modern medicine—and on the reputation of Cleveland Clinic as the world leader in heart care. Dr. Sones's discovery illustrates *opportunistic innovation* because his work exemplifies the intersection of serendipity and the prepared mind.

The aorta is the major vessel carrying blood away from the beating heart to nourish the rest of the body. Just after blood is ejected from the left heart chamber (the ventricle), smaller conduits, the coronary arteries, carry blood to the heart itself to keep the dynamic muscle alive.

Prior to 1958, direct imaging of the coronary arteries had not been attempted. In fact, it was believed that direct dye injection into these small arteries would cause sudden death. The Nobel laureate in 1956 for discoveries concerning heart catheterization, André F. Cournand, declared in 1950 that no physician should ever perform such a procedure.

Dr. Sones was a cardiac and aortic imaging expert. In October 1958, in his Cleveland Clinic basement laboratory, Sones was supervising trainee Royston C. Lewis in the study of a 26-year-old patient with rheumatic fever, a common malady of the time resulting from untreated streptococcal infections. Performing the angiography procedure was a two-person job: one physician threaded the tube into position in the circulatory system and prepared to inject the radiopaque dye that filled and defined the vessels, while the second manned the imaging screen sunk beneath the exam table in a pit. Neither physician could see what the other was doing.

That day, Dr. Sones was viewing the beating heart and great vessels through a periscope, while Dr. Lewis was positioning the hollow tube to deliver 50 cc of dye into the heart chambers and aorta, or so he intended. Instead, the catheter moved just a millimeter or two, which caused the dye to be delivered not into the capacious ventricle, but directly into the small-caliber coronary artery system. The bolus of dye injected into such a small vessel stopped the patient's heart, but not before Dr. Sones witnessed the first elucidation of the coronary artery system by direct cannulation.

A happy ending was ensured when Dr. Sones restarted the patient's heart within seconds. A new era in heart and vascular diagnostics was begun, with this discovery leading to greater understanding of coronary anatomy, physiology, and pathology.

Dr. Sones subsequently collaborated with René G. Favaloro, a young Argentinian cardiovascular surgeon visiting Cleveland Clinic to hone his craft, to perform the first coronary artery bypass grafting (CABG). Prior to CABG, patients who suffered a heart attack were treated symptomatically with rest and pain medication, and the morbidity and mortality rates were unacceptably high. Although the frequency of CABG has decreased by nearly 50 percent in the past decade due to less-invasive alternatives, it still accounts for almost 2 percent of all annual U.S. operations, a number exceeding 200,000.[3]

In a letter some three decades later to fellow world-renowned cardiologist J. Willis Hurst, Dr. Sones reflected on the aftermath of the inaugural incident: "During the ensuing days, I began to think that this accident might point the way for the development of a technique which was exactly what we had been seeking." An accident? This is a prime illustration of opportunistic innovation.

The Mason Sones example contains the two key elements essential for opportunistic innovation: a fertile environment and an opportune event. Opportunistic innovation is different from a so-called innovation "lightning strike," because in that situation, prevailing randomness may not permit the germinal action to be witnessed or experienced by the appropriate agent.

A common lament when describing a medical diagnostic challenge is that the key piece of data "may have seen me, but I did not see it." Some barrier prevents the eureka moment from occurring. Maybe it's a knowledge gap. Perhaps the glimpse is experienced out of context or at a time of distraction or fatigue. Or maybe there's just too much noise surrounding the would-be innovator because he or she is buried beneath the mundane or irrelevant.

Here's the implication for mission-driven innovation champions and the institutional functions they lead regarding opportunistic innovation: it's your responsibility to optimize the setting around your creatives and inform them of the benefits of perpetual preparedness to discover.

Expertise is ubiquitous around us; you must trust that each of your colleagues is as knowledgeable in their craft as you are. They know the unmet needs and where pressure points exist and very likely are presented with novel solutions. Make sure your associates are engaged thinkers who know how to recognize solutions that will make a difference. In addition, ensure that your would-be innovators are comfortable about engaging in your process and that it's easy to do so. The moment may be fleeting when the right problem and the right innovator intersect; being equipped to receive the novel solution and run with it is the purview of the effective innovation function.

Recommendations to inspire and capture opportunistic innovation include:

- Continually remind your colleagues that everyone is an expert and an innovator. Keep innovation top of mind and foster connectivity by holding specific events throughout the year and by creating a site for information exchange on your institution's intranet.

- Educate your organization about the powerful, yet ephemeral nature of creative thought. Encourage colleagues to record their aha moments. Provide simple tools to promote this activity, such as small notebooks. Have paper napkins at meal functions that carry the message and the metaphor; encourage attendees to flip the napkins over and note their burgeoning ideas.

- Ensure that your idea development process is easy to access and nonthreatening to the inventor. We don't advocate a one-size-fits-all or black-box approach for opportunistic innovation.

Second-Degree Innovation: Organic

One of the reasons I have the best job in all of healthcare is that I work at a physician-led institution where the CEO is one of the world's foremost proponents of medical innovation. Toby Cosgrove is not only a highly respected medical executive, he's a fellow surgeon and prolific inventor holding more than 30 patents. Before taking the helm of Cleveland Clinic, Dr. Cosgrove performed some 22,000 cardiac surgeries, and he has authored nearly 450 scholarly articles and book chapters. Treating disorders of the heart's mitral valve is among his fortes. Dr. Cosgrove is an example of an organic innovator.

The importance of the mitral valve cannot be underestimated. Blood is collected in the upper chamber of the heart, the right atrium, after delivering its precious cargo, oxygen, to tissues all over the body. Before the right ventricle propels blood to the lungs to reload oxygen for another round, the blood transits through the mitral valve. If damaged by disease or disorder, the valve can become floppy, rendering it inefficient in its work guarding the aperture between the two chambers. The results can be benign, such as a heart murmur, a nuisance to be explained each time you get a physical, or it can be life-threatening.

A structure as delicate as the mitral valve is challenging to reconstruct. Even the skilled surgeon encounters difficulty in achieving the right balance between flexibility and tautness—and remember, the heart is beating during this technical exercise!

Drawing on a design reminiscent of his wife's embroidery hoop, Dr. Cosgrove figured out that by employing a cloth-covered, semicircular spring device called an annuloplasty ring, the mitral valve could be repaired predictably with lower complication rates. This device put capability in the hands of many surgeons and improved the lives of thousands. It represents *organic innovation* at its finest.

Organic innovation arises when experts, in the course of their frontline experiences, recognize ways to advance their craft. It's the workhorse of all mission-driven innovation. In many ways, it's the most important and fundamental form of reducing transcendent thought to practice. It's often the most hard-won, but also the stickiest and most sustainable. Organic innovation is the most common type of creative thought generation and the one around which every innovation function or technology transfer office must build its infrastructure.

At Cleveland Clinic, every specialty is replete with one or more colleagues considered among the world's experts, and each vertical care delivery unit (we call them institutes) maintains a deep bench. The collaboration with fellow experts that is so catalytic to innovation is a distinctive strength of the Cleveland Clinic community. It's a great place to practice and innovate because none of us perceive we're alone in being at the top of our game, and there is never a barrier to seeking the opinion of another maven practicing alongside us.

Two issues require clarification and differentiation from opportunistic innovation. First, just because organic innovation is the blocking and tackling of innovation does not automatically imply that organic innovation is incremental. In fact, organic innovation can be disruptive.

Second, the distinction between opportunistic and organic innovation is that the former is a spark, the proverbial lit match that lands in the gasoline shed. The latter is the smoldering ember that finally reaches the right temperature and conditions to ignite evident and actionable breakthrough. Both opportunistic and organic innovation can feature the same elements, human and otherwise. But the essential catalyst for the opportunistic innovator is attentiveness to the unexpected, while the organic innovator mines ideas over time through ceaseless exposure.

It shouldn't be surprising that opportunistic and organic innovation track together. The most experienced people are often the most prepared to recognize and accept the unique stimulus.

Recommendations to inspire and capture organic innovation include:

- Cultivate frequent contact with your most experienced personnel and prolific innovators. From casual lunches to recurring meetings, hearing what the experts see, think, hear, and say is valuable to an innovation team.

- Maintain the crucial processes that propel innovation through the virtuous cycle.

- Be a proponent for innovation in its most basic form, both inside and outside of your institution or organization.

Third-Degree Innovation: Synthetic

Synthetic innovation reflects the belief that innovation occurs best at the intersection of domains. Whether the commodity is knowledge, experience, resources, relationships, or even culture, uniting creative people and institutions is one of the most catalytic ways to advance innovation. Furthermore, allowing creatives to bring their life experiences into medical innovation can also pay dividends.

Innovation can come from a doctor-patient interaction at the bedside, a research inspiration at the laboratory bench, or seemingly out of thin air. When Anesthesia Institute chair David L. Brown, a general aviation and former military pilot, was making a cross-country flight, the advanced avionics controlling his plane inspired him to conceive a novel system to help manage patients' anesthesia needs during surgery.

Much like a pilot, an anesthesiologist relies on numerous complex factors to keep patients safe while in the medically induced state that allows surgery to be performed painlessly and without recollection. Anesthesiologists, however, didn't have computers or control towers to help guide clinicians to the correct decisions. In addition, complex surgeries can take many hours, and as is the case with all humans, clinicians are subject to fatigue and distraction.

Computers don't have these stresses and are great vigilance monitors. Dr. Brown invented Decision Support Systems (DSS), which amplified physician judgment and increased capacity to manage multiple patients. DSS is like a tap on the shoulder to keep clinicians ahead of the case, providing anesthesia staff with an extra set of eyes and extensive cognitive processing power both to improve clinical and management decision making in the perioperative environment and to allow anesthesiologists to react more rapidly to potentially harmful trends.

DSS was commercialized and further developed by CCI's ninth spin-off health information technology (HIT) company, Talis Clinical, LLC. The DSS platform has been combined with additional HIT tools to help manage patients in other acute care settings. The volume of hospitals, clinicians, and patients this technology benefits is remarkable.

Dr. Brown's contribution exemplifies one form of synthetic innovation, in which the inventor removes partitions in his brain to allow mingling of experiences and expertise. When inventors feel that freedom to ideate, the job of the innovation leader is to remove roadblocks.

Cleveland Clinic's most tangible expression of synthetic innovation at work on an institutional scale has been the Global Healthcare Innovations Alliance (GHIA), the largest consortium of academic medical centers (AMCs), research universities, and aligned corporate partners dedicated to mission-driven innovation. The alliance has paid dividends in co-invention and sharing of innovation culture.

Recommendations to inspire and capture synthetic innovation include:

- Cross-pollinate within your own organization, across the street, across the country, or around the globe.

- Be proactive about defining the rules by which partnerships will be executed, including joint management agreements and definitions on how ownership and distributions will be executed.

- Consider relationships with organizations that don't look like you. Whether bringing together urban and rural hospitals or combining healthcare entities with industrial giants, concentrate less on what each party does and more on how and why they do it. When you ensure cultural alignment first, complementary and supplementary facets are much easier to identify.

■ Don't try to advantage yourself or your institution against a potential or secured partner. It will either be obvious from the outset and derail the relationship or will besmirch your reputation when discovered and forever going forward.

Fourth-Degree Innovation: Geographic

A compelling example of geographic innovation is the partnership CCI developed with Parker Hannifin Corp. For those unfamiliar with Parker, chances are the company's products have touched you, or vice versa, multiple times today, especially if you drove in a car, flew in a plane, or operated a machine. Parker is a Cleveland-based motion-control giant that solves some of the world's most challenging engineering problems.

When we sat down to explore whether there was commonality on which to build a sustainable relationship, there was an initial polite but palpable level of incredulity in the room. To paraphrase Parker executives, "I'm not sure that you would be interested in what we do. We solve problems such as getting fluids to flow through tubes with valves in them." CCI responded, "That's exactly what our cardiologists and urologists do." Since those initial meetings, we've built a robust medical device portfolio with Parker and a valuable intellectual property (IP) estate through co-innovation.

I've had many of my best ideas in orthopaedic device development walking through the hardware store. Translocating an idea—even existing technology—for use in an entirely different discipline is also an expression of geographic innovation.

Another expression of geographic innovation is attracting successful innovators who have never resided in our sphere into medical innovation to leverage their talents to help patients. That's what we did with our hugely successful spin-off company, Explorys, which was recently purchased by IBM's Watson Group.

Big data is big news these days, and Explorys is one of the leaders in harnessing a powerful, secure software platform to provide near-instantaneous answers that ultimately lead to better treatment, enhanced access, and lower cost. Explorys can examine its 315 billion data points from a population health perspective or do a deep dive into a single patient's medical record. There is amazing potential for clinical care delivery and research.

One would think that cofounders Stephen McHale and Charlie Lougheed spent decades in and around hospitals to garner the depth of understanding required to bring such a powerful tool to healthcare, but not so. These computer geniuses came from the worlds of banking, defense, and telecom, where facility with big data has thrived for years. Their association with cofounder and Cleveland Clinic physician Anil Jain and CCI "took them to medical school." The result was a unique archival and analytic tool that logically fits in healthcare but might have been sequestered outside of the sector if not for geographic innovation.

Explorys was acquired by IBM's amazing Watson Healthcare team in early 2015 after CCI spun off the company in 2009. At the time of the IBM acquisition, Explorys neared 150 employees and had curated anonymized records on more than 50 million patients in databases that can be mined to gain insight on activities ranging from medical research to care delivery.

Healthcare is trending up toward 20 percent of the U.S. gross domestic product. If a company isn't already in healthcare, it's trying to get in, or at least considering it. The most successful mission-driven innovation organizations in healthcare will be portals of bilateral information flow that enhances the creative potential of both the medical sector and nontraditional partners from outside healthcare. This will include adapting existing consumer technology to medical applications and vice versa, or promoting collaboration. In either case, visionary institutions will act as the stewards that translocate people, technology, or both between adjacent or even remote sectors.

Recommendations to inspire and capture geographic innovation include:

- Keep your eyes open. Just as a great athlete in one sport can appreciate the level of mastery of another in his or her own sport, recognize a disruptive technology or breakthrough idea when you see it, regardless of the sphere.

- Actively solicit ideas and critical analysis from respected innovators in different disciplines. Fresh thinking and a worldview unencumbered by historical interaction may provide just the insight needed to propel an innovation to new heights. Remember, innovation happens best at the intersection of knowledge domains.

- Appreciate the power of platform technologies— those capabilities that can be employed in different scenarios and circumstances.

Fifth-Degree Innovation: Strategic

Cleveland Clinic is always searching for greater ways to fulfill its mission to provide better care of the sick, investigation into their problems, and further education of those who serve. Having just mentioned IBM with respect to geographic innovation, one of the company's shared values as an organization is to pursue "Innovation that matters, for our company and for the world."[4] When IBM leadership identified the Watson supercomputer as promising a significant difference in medicine, Cleveland Clinic explored a strategic innovation relationship that would leverage the strengths and resources of both organizations.

Beginning in 2002, Cleveland Clinic was an early adopter of electronic medical records. While we strive to remain in the forefront of managing healthcare informatics, challenges have expanded as the body of patient data multiplies exponentially. In addition, our physicians struggle to keep up with the explosion of medical information, which doubles every 18 months. We needed a computing partner to help.

Similarly, IBM needed a healthcare partner to leverage Watson's cognitive computing, voice recognition, and machine learning capacities to extract pertinent data from the ever-increasing medical literature and simultaneously sift through individual clinical records with a speed and sensitivity exceeding the capability of the caregiver.

For a problem of this scope and impact, it would be hard to find a better correspondence of needs, complementary resource inventory, and understanding of potential barriers. What might have been an exceedingly complex engagement was reduced to the comparatively simple assignment to innovate around specific needs that had been already identified by market leaders using best practices—that is the essence of *strategic innovation*.

Strategic innovation is the holy grail of the practice; it increases efficiency and accelerates results. Strategic innovation also reduces variables and streamlines the creative development process. Laser-like focus on technology or solution development that fills a recognized need, usually of an eagerly waiting consumer base or partner, is an additional hallmark of strategic innovation. Strategic innovation takes an endeavor typically characterized by frequent failure and challenging algorithmic decision making and makes it more linear, while removing the ambiguity of whether the market will adopt the solutions.

Strategic innovation is the inverse of opportunistic innovation. The latter is a passive rebound of new knowledge that comes the way of the innovator in an unanticipated circumstance. The former starts with collected expertise and robust resources ready to pounce on an already-identified market need.

Another example of strategic innovation is our spin-off CardioMEMS, Inc. With our heart program ranked as best in the nation for 20 consecutive years by *U.S. News & World Report*, Cleveland Clinic has a strategic priority to continually develop lifesaving cardiovascular technologies. In development of the CardioMEMS system for treating congestive heart failure (CHF), we had three imperatives: (1) replace pharmacologic treatments with a medical device solution, (2) utilize microelectromechanical systems (MEMS) technology, essentially extremely small devices, and (3) find applicability to additional problems.

The CardioMEMS technology was developed by collaborators from Cleveland Clinic and Georgia Institute of Technology. While always targeting treatment of CHF, the technology was first used to sense leaks when an endovascular graft was implanted during abdominal aortic aneurism surgery. Once proof of concept was established with that application, CardioMEMS advanced to its primary objective of managing CHF patients without hospitalization.

A sensor the size of a small paper clip is permanently placed in the pulmonary artery to monitor pressure. Patients take a daily reading from home and send the information to their doctor, who can adjust medication as needed. Previously, such patients would frequently be hospitalized—usually in the intensive care unit—to treat the condition pharmacologically.

St. Jude Medical, Inc., saw the value and purchased an initial $60 million stake in CardioMEMS. Four years later, the company was fully acquired by the global medical technology leader for $375 million.

The development and divestment of CardioMEMS represents the hallmark of strategic innovation: solution development that fills a recognized need among eagerly awaiting customers. The result was introduction of a bold new technology, the first of its kind for treatment of CHF, and its commercial success has been profound.

There is both synergy and synchronicity expressed in strategic innovation that differentiate it from synthetic innovation and build on its foundation. Individuals or institutions aren't simply joining forces, pooling resources, and comparing notes. Strategic innovation is set in motion by a mature system of problem identification and by market readiness to adopt novel, customized answers.

Recommendations to inspire and capture strategic innovation include:

- Establish close relationships with your divestment and transactional partners. Do as much as you can to identify their unmet needs, and then leverage your creative minds to meet the challenges.

- While taking care not to diminish opportunistic and organic innovation, assemble multifunctional teams of experts to participate in structured ideation sessions around specific, market-generated opportunities.

- Maintain a list of high-concept, high-impact problems that we all should be pursuing. This innovation bucket list may never be fully achieved but will stimulate the minds of your creatives.

Sixth-Degree Innovation: Telescopic

In 2014, more than 230,000 new U.S. cases of invasive breast cancer were expected, with an additional 62,000-plus new cases of noninvasive (in situ) breast cancer. One in eight U.S. women will be diagnosed with breast cancer during their lifetime.[5]

If these statistics reflect the numbers *afflicted* by breast cancer, 100 percent of us are *affected* by this pervasive disease. I have yet to meet someone who doesn't have a loved one or friend who has been touched by breast cancer.

Vincent K. Tuohy is a talented and visionary scientist at Cleveland Clinic's Lerner Research Institute who turned his interests to the prevention of breast cancer. He determined that a specific protein expressed in breast cancer patients was not present in healthy women. From his scientific foundation in immunology, he recognized that the immune system works best at controlling pathologic entities when it can concentrate on prevention and not play catch-up after the disease process has taken hold.

The result is a promising breast cancer vaccine. While the rest of clinical and academic medicine was focused on breast cancer treatment, taking the typical weapons of drugs and surgery into battle, Dr. Tuohy thought differently about the problem to establish a new discipline: adult vaccination against aging-related tumors such as breast, ovarian, and prostate tumors. The implications may be far-reaching. Dr. Tuohy's new idea has garnered support from members of the philanthropic community touched by breast cancer who want to see the disease eradicated, and CCI spun off a company, Shield Biotech, to further the commercial possibilities associated with this discovery science. Dr. Tuohy's vaccine is still in early clinical trials and may not be available for a decade.

Similar to Dr. Tuohy, Stanley L. Hazen looked in a different direction, but also looked further and forever changed our understanding of the link between diet and heart disease. Ask virtually anyone about the relationship between eating red meat and developing artery-clogging, cholesterol-derived plaques that limit blood flow to the heart, and he or she will espouse a direct correlation. Even answers from the nutrition and scientific communities would point to excess saturated fat in the diet.

As Dr. Hazen's work has shown, this blame may be misplaced. It appears that a bacterium in the gut of those who regularly eat eggs, meat, and other animal products readily converts nutrients in those foods to compounds that play a significant role in the evolution of heart disease. In an ingenious experiment, Dr. Hazen and colleagues gave vegetarians and vegans a chemical found abundantly in red meat and dairy products (L-carnitine) and followed the subsequent production of a related compound trimethylamine N-oxide (TMAO) known to alter the metabolism of cholesterol, curtailing its removal from the bloodstream.

Dr. Hazen recognized that there is a completely different bacterial population in the intestinal tracts of meat eaters and vegetarians or vegans. Even when the non–meat eaters were loaded up with L-carnitine—and some even crossed the line and ate meat—they still didn't manifest increased levels of TMAO in the short term. Ushering in broad transformational thinking—not only in this field but across many disciplines—is recognition that gut microflora may be the key to unlocking disease processes.

Cleveland Clinic and its spin-off Cleveland HeartLab, Inc. recently announced a collaboration with Procter & Gamble to develop and commercialize a diagnostic and management solution. Cleveland HeartLab will develop a test to measure blood levels of TMAO, while Cleveland Clinic researchers will work with Procter & Gamble to develop an over-the-counter product to help manage TMAO levels.

Innovation is like optics. Opportunistic innovators transition from being *creative* to becoming *inventive* by seeing a
shooting star. Organic innovators look through a microscope
to see how incremental improvements in techniques or technologies can have a magnified impact.

Telescopic innovation embodies two concepts: these innovators literally look through a different lens at problems and
solutions, and they combine intelligence with insight to see
solutions to big problems in greater detail than others. While
their ideas may initially seem like innovation from another
planet, entire disciplines subsequently pivot to follow these
pioneers. There's a viral effect as breakthroughs proliferate.

Is Your Organization
Prepared to Innovate?

It's true that innovation—in at least one, if not all of the six
degrees—is occurring throughout your organization. But
making the most of your organization's inherent innovation
is a challenging endeavor. There must be institutional preparedness to tackle, sustain, and scale innovation.

Before the mantle of "innovative" can be bestowed, an
organization must succeed at getting technology developments across the finish line and into the market, or growing
the institutional brand by monetizing a core competency
through consulting or another form of dissemination of IP.

How is preparedness for innovation determined? Typically, managers compare current and historical data to
evaluate where their organization stands, an example being
comparison of prior-year and actual financials. A similar "retrospectoscope" is employed to benchmark against
regional or even national clinical practice competitors, such
as comparing number of new patients seen or amount of
funded research.

While there's no doubt that looking in the rearview mirror can be a logical and useful operations management exercise, evaluating innovation capability is not exactly like calculating EBITDA. Assessing innovation readiness or measuring innovation output demands a balance—contemplating the rearview, but spending most of the time peering through the expansive windshield.

As Cleveland Clinic has organically grown its innovation function over the past two decades, we've been pioneers. CCI trailblazers embarked upon the journey without a map and with few other institutions against which to measure our plans or progress. Out of necessity, we had to find a way to examine our own performance and the characteristics of other institutions to determine their present and future promise in this field.

It isn't reasonable to expect that those running your P&L will automatically share your level of enthusiasm for the part innovation could play in your organization's future. Recalling that innovation is nonlinear, can be painfully inefficient, and is failure-laden, how can you blame your CFO for getting nervous when you present these factors as normal? Innovation leaders can't simply ignore requests for data-driven confirmation that they are providing value and executing optimally, despite the normal headwinds that face our practice. The scrutiny directed to performance reporting is greater now than at any time in history because of financial pressures placed on all healthcare organizations (or universities or commercial businesses).

Thus, there's a growing demand on the part of C-suite executives to measure organizational preparedness to enter into or excel in innovation. Despite the fact that innovation can be expensive and carries with it a high failure rate, practically everyone wants to be in the game. Organizations must consider innovation investment, which has greater inherent risk and delayed reward, against the resource requirements of their core, which delivers incremental growth. Today's healthcare decisions must be data-driven; for innovation-related metrics, this means technical, cultural, and economic data.

Leaders now have a choice about diving into the deep end of the innovation pool—is it a buy or a build? Stated alternatively, should they seek a partner or go it alone and build an innovation function from scratch? As institutional pioneers in innovation, and as originator of the GHIA, we assumed responsibility for developing instruments to conduct the right inquiry and glean the right information for decisions about innovation execution. In the process, we discovered the optimal way to validate our own practice and choose the best partners for our growing alliance. Following are the tools we developed and employ to evaluate institutional innovation capability and culture.

The Innovation Global Practice Survey (*i*GPS)

The scholarly literature is dotted with reports detailing innovation capability maturity models (ICMM). These instruments began to emerge in the late 1980s and throughout the 1990s, designed primarily by software engineering concerns, such as the Software Engineering Institute, and sometimes funded by government agencies, including the Department of Defense. ICMMs started to gain more traction in the 2000s, owing to increased scientific rigor and applicability to contemporary R&D functions.

In 2010, CCI's growth in size, scope, and level of success required us to think more critically about our own cultural and operational assets. We were also experiencing a growing demand to assist AMCs, research universities, and nontraditional partners in industry and government in maximizing their innovation potential.

For these reasons, we sought guidelines from the existing literature, but we strongly believed that industrial models for interrogating innovation capability were not directly applicable to healthcare- and bioscience-sector institutions. Naturally, we sought to fill the void. Not only did CCI need a valid instrument for introspection and benchmarking of our existing function, many of our partners in mission-driven innovation needed one as well to help determine if and how they might enter the innovation ecosystem.

The result was CCI's Innovation Global Practice Survey (*i*GPS), a suite of diagnostic instruments that yields objective and subjective data about an institution's past, present, and future innovation capabilities. Our tool is designed to assess past activity, highlight current status, and forecast future success. It is best when deployed broadly across an organization from the C-suite to the frontline innovator to evaluate the entire organization's preparedness to innovate. It provides leaders with a playbook that identifies core competencies, practice efficiencies, optimization opportunities, and potential collaborators. The *i*GPS can be used to track an organization's growth trajectory or benchmark the organization against its peers of similar size and composition.

The utility of the *i*GPS resides in its disciplined methodology and ability to reduce variables to metrics. We identified the right variables, quantified them, and weighed the relative importance of selected characteristics. The level of specificity permits innovation leaders to inventory, recognize, rate, and prioritize opportunities. Strategies for improvement in selected parameters can then be furnished by collaboration or consultation.

The components of the *i*GPS range from the concrete descriptors of innovation architecture to the cultural characteristics that reveal the amount of innovation DNA that resides within an organization. We have validated the instruments through thousands of hours of assembly, interview, analysis, and reporting. The insight gleaned by utilizing the *i*GPS, as opposed to an undisciplined cursory assessment, has allowed CCI to be a better partner and choose better partners.

The *i*GPS has four individual components. Each is described in turn.

- The Innovation Infrastructure Inquiry (3*i*)
- The Medical Innovation Maturity Survey (M*i*MS)
- The Graded Perspective Analysis (GPA)
- Business Engineering (BE)

The sum of these parts has proven to be a valuable 360-degree evaluation of an organization's place in the innovation universe. As demand grows for institutional leaders to set the innovation course for their holdings, proven tools like the *i*GPS will be even more valuable.

The Innovation Infrastructure Inquiry (3i)

CCI developed a survey to assess innovation architecture, which we termed, appropriately, Innovation Infrastructure Inquiry (3*i*). It has become the foundation upon which we build our more sophisticated evaluations.

There are three primary factors to be monitored and maximized to achieve a satisfactory score or rating on 3*i*: (1) dedicated innovation resources, (2) commercialization processes, and (3) favorable innovation outcome metrics. Additional factors may augment these basics, but without this foundation even the most prolific engines of transcendent thought will prove unsuccessful in presenting solutions to the marketplace.

In 2013, CCI invited dozens of AMCs and research universities to participate in the 3*i* survey to catalog their innovation profiles. Questions related to licensing revenue, invention disclosures, licenses executed, startups created, patents filed and issued, and commercialization budgets and infrastructure. Results were published in the *Medical Innovation Playbook*, a CCI publication in collaboration with the Council for American Medical Innovation.[6]

Perusing the *Playbook* gives an institution's innovation leadership a contemporary scorecard that can be used to evaluate and optimize their functions. The goal was not to rank programs or even identify best practices. The goal was to create an unprecedented catalog of the commitment to innovation and present success in delivering breakthrough biomedical advancements.

The reported components also include human and financial resources dedicated to innovation, domains in which creative thought is developing, structure and operation of technology transfer units, and how commercial proceeds are distributed. Following is a summary of the survey results that informed the *Playbook*. Individual institutional profiles are detailed in the publication.

Operational Characteristics

The overwhelming majority of technology commercialization offices (TCOs) operate as a subsidiary of their parent organizations. Only about 10 percent of innovation functions are independent, some as for-profit spin-offs. This is the structural manifestation of the mission-driven innovation philosophy.

The number of TCOs that derive their funding solely from a direct budget line item in their organization's P&L is roughly equivalent to those that diversify their funding sources by reinvesting their commercialization revenues (39 percent versus 35 percent). Government grants and various forms of philanthropy are becoming increasingly important to resourcing innovation functions.

One of the distinguishing characteristics of success-ful mission-driven innovation entities is the commitment to internalize the core capabilities that advance creative thought. In order to translate technologies to the market-place, proof-of-concept funding is required to accomplish legal, engineering, prototyping, and transactional milestones. Approximately two-thirds of *Playbook* respondents maintain a dedicated budget for these developmental investments.

Average operating budget per full-time equivalent dedi-cated to innovation and commercialization is about $232,000 and relatively consistent across the cohort. Twenty-five percent of respondents have an executive or entrepreneur in residence (EIR), a seasoned business expert who may be between opportunities after an early exit and coaches the young innovators and business builders. Some EIRs donate their time or are paid a salary, while others negotiate for equity in the evolving companies they mentor.

Nonprofits can and should engage in the creation of com-panies that reinforce their mission to improve and extend human life. Some 85 percent of *Playbook* respondents are at least partially involved in incubation, with 49 percent being the sole entity engaged in startup gestation. Nearly 60 percent of the institutions polled have developed institutional incu-bators or accelerators to augment the chances for success of nascent companies.

Portfolio Characteristics

HEALTHCARE-RELATED ACTIVITY AS A PERCENT OF KEY COMMERCIALIZATION METRICS

The *Playbook* cataloged the combined innovation activity of more than 65 AMCs and research universities. This created an overview of nearly 10,000 invention disclosures, 6,400 patent applications, and almost 2,000 issued patents. These translated into 2,600 royalty-bearing licenses, 280 spin-off companies, and \$1.5 billion in healthcare/bioscience commercialization revenue. TCOs or innovation functions on the campuses of healthcare systems dedicated essentially their entire commercialization efforts to medical innovation, while multidisciplinary TCOs attribute approximately two-thirds of their commercialization activity to healthcare.

HEALTHCARE INVENTION DOMAIN DISTRIBUTION
Institutions have distinct capabilities and characteristics and direct their innovation activity accordingly. The typical portfolio includes medical devices, drugs and other "molecules" (diagnostics, biologics, and research assays), and HIT. Many progressive institutions also have developed mechanisms by which the know-how and experience resulting from core functions can be monetized. At Cleveland Clinic, we call this *delivery solutions*. Many delivery solutions are enabled by HIT platforms.

For example, Cleveland Clinic has traditionally been a strong surgical institution, especially in highly technical subspecialties. This forte also reflects the ethos of the industrial Midwest, which has long been a leader in advanced manufacturing. Therefore, it should be no surprise that medical device innovation, as reported in the *Playbook*, dominated CCI's portfolio at 58 percent.

Since the *Playbook* was published, Cleveland Clinic's portfolio has grown in number, but it has also broadened in distribution with the amazing growth trajectory of HIT advancements and greater equality between the major technology domains as percentage of invention disclosure. (See Figure 6.1.)

FIGURE 6.1 Healthcare Invention Disclosures by Type. Healthcare invention disclosure by domain among the 60-plus institutions reporting in Cleveland Clinic's *Medical Innovation Playbook.*

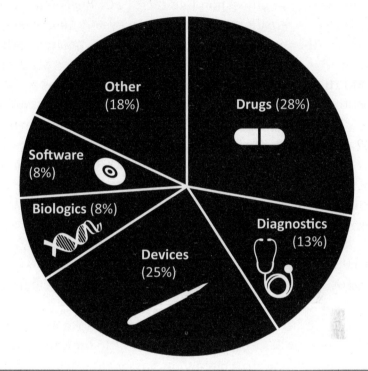

The Medical Innovation Maturity Survey (MiMS) and Graded Perspective Analysis (GPA)

Innovation can be among the most powerful forces defining individual or institutional success, yet it remains mysterious to many contemporary leaders. C-suite executives know they want their organizations to be innovative and good at it, but many can't quite get a handle on their own innovation identities.

Recall that every patent or product, each invention and industry, started with an innovation. The question facing

C-suite leaders, and especially chief innovation officers, is how to cultivate and sustain innovation to create competitive advantage and serve enterprise mission. How do leaders instill or inspire innovation into their individual colleagues and make its pursuit an enterprise priority and competency?

How the transcendent idea set forth by a creative individual or team is handled makes the difference between delivering a game-changing advancement that helps people (and makes money) and one that fizzles unrequited. It sounds a bit like the age-old nature-versus-nurture debate, parsing the contribution of objective assets like personnel and process against delicate cultural characteristics. Cleveland Clinic believes the correct answer is a hybrid. But we also seek to minimize the frustration and variability associated with balancing the encoded with the elusive.

One of the core competencies that have allowed CCI to grow and succeed is our development of and adherence to disciplined processes to gestate ideas. But we also benefit from a unique environment in which these promising concepts mature. To better understand our own culture and to help colleagues similarly desiring to contribute to the knowledge-based, innovation-driven economy, we sought to better define medical innovation maturity on an institutional level.

We began by building consensus around a working definition of innovation maturity. Our group of professionals from all facets of the innovation community collaborated on the following:

Medical innovation maturity reflects the level to which an organization fosters, supports, and capitalizes on the structural and cultural assets and capabilities associated with developing creative thought to tangible outcomes for the purpose of achieving mission-related goals.

With the foundation in place, we sought to make the assessment of organizational preparedness to innovate in healthcare and the biosciences as objective as possible. The result was our proprietary Medical Innovation Maturity Survey. This simplistically elegant, yet comprehensive instrument interrogates institutional leaders, scholars, and inventors across multiple dimensions of innovation-related variables. The responses are weighted according to their importance and impact on the innovation practice. The utility of the MiMS results from its ability to identify the present status of the innovation culture and recognize pathways to improvement in specific elements or engagements.

The MiMS instrument yields a numerical score (0 to 100) with corresponding subsection scores in three fields: people, process, and philosophy. (See Appendix C for a sample scoring.) Subordinate to the three fields are 17 dimensions that compose a complex mosaic defining innovation in space and time. The process is highly analytical, with a focus on understanding the philosophical and aspirational objectives of all stakeholders who use or influence the innovation infrastructure. The scored survey transforms subjective responses into objective data through the carefully constructed cross-referencing and weighting systems built into the tool. The final score is correlated to a level of innovation maturity that we delineate as *entering, engaging, emerging, excelling,* or *extending.*

The MiMS is a 360-degree evaluation of innovation. We've found it to be an indispensable tool in three ways. First, it fosters consistent improvement of Cleveland Clinic's own culture of innovation. Second, it promotes the ability to optimize the GHIA by assisting our existing partners. Finally, it expands our portfolio of offerings to organizations aspiring to participate in the formalized practice of innovation by helping them understand their current status and future potential.

The first cousin and complementary tool of M*i*MS is the Graded Perspective Analysis (GPA). Aptly named because it applies a letter grade (A–F) derived from the traditional 4.0 scale, the GPA scores the free responses to 10 questions carefully designed to supplement the data gleaned during the M*i*MS. (See sidebar.) These questions address categories—definition, aspiration, status, legacy, opportunity, responsibility, barriers, recognition, collaboration, and economic development—that contribute to a comprehensive commercialization ecosystem.

Aside from the letter or numerical grade, however, one of the other benefits of the GPA is that it provides direct quotes from innovation stakeholders that can be very informative to those leading or analyzing an innovation effort. In a broader assessment, anonymous quotes can still be related, but ascribed to the interviewee's level at the organization. For example, alignment or discord between C-suite executives and frontline innovators can be discerned easily through their quotes.

Although the M*i*MS and the GPA are designed as companion pieces, the GPA can be used alone as a conversation starter around innovation with the uninitiated. It has cultivated a deeper understanding of how intrinsic innovation has become in organizations with mature practices.

The combination of M*i*MS and GPA has put a very valuable arrow in CCI's quiver. With these additional results sitting beside the 3*i*, we can now uncover the previously invisible elements that define the culture of innovation in a healthcare or academic enterprise, or throughout a network of organizations such as the GHIA. Perhaps just as important, armed with identification of specific areas of strength and weakness, CCI can now pick and promote partners in ways that were heretofore unavailable.

GRADED PERSPECTIVE ANALYSIS (GPA) QUESTIONS

1. What does the term "innovation" mean to you?
2. Why should your organization/institution innovate?
3. Would you characterize your organization/institution as a "high innovation" environment? (Please explain.)
   A) What are the most impactful innovations that your organization/institution has contributed over its history?
   B) What are the most impactful innovations that your organization/institution has contributed over the past two decades?
4. Where do the greatest opportunities to innovate lie in modern healthcare?
5. Is innovation the purview of industry, academic medical centers (AMCs) and research universities, or both?
6. What are the barriers to innovation in AMCs and research universities?
7. How should innovators in AMCs and research universities be rewarded/compensated?
8. What role does collaboration play in fostering innovation?
9. How does your institution view its role in regional economic development, and how is it related to company attraction and retention?

Innovation culture is thought to be more like an art, but we have endeavored to add as much science to its assessment as we can. We don't interfere with the creative process, we interrogate it. These tools have allowed us to bring innovation maturity out of the shadows and into the light, where it can grow and develop into an asset to be managed and shared to better serve the enterprise missions.

Business Engineering (BE)

Business Engineering (BE) completes the quartet of assessment tools under the *i*GPS umbrella, tools that have empowered CCI to become not only a leading practitioner of mission-driven innovation but also its major purveyor. BE was established to wed entrepreneurial ideas developed outside of our institution or in the GHIA with CCI's experience in spinning off more than 70 companies. Cleveland Clinic believes providing fledgling prerevenue or early revenue companies with access to its expertise will accelerate market entry and adoption of innovations. Further, the potential to marry elements of our large aggregated IP portfolio to an early or incomplete commercial concern could position our BE clients for sustainable success, thus improving patient care on a global scale.

Opening the BE funnel as an access point to our normal operating platform is logical. We have considerable proficiency in bringing the technologies of our institution and partners to the marketplace, so why not permit access to ideas that gestated outside of our consortium? The offerings of BE include, but are not limited to:

- IP review and management

- Access to key opinion leaders

- Business plan support

- Leadership and governance identification

- Market analysis and validation

- Incubation mentorship

- Financial/financing assessment

- Clinical validation

CCI realizes many benefits from engagement in BE. Chief among them is to refresh our enthusiasm through exposure to the zeal of the outside entrepreneurs who share the mission to extend and improve human life.

In more concrete terms, two facets stand out as the reasons behind opening the aperture to our process and engaging in "intake" rather than just "output." First, we're already engaged in the development of spin-off companies; why not get a head start by associating with companies that have moved through the development cycle, albeit from external ideas? Second, the chance to cross-pollinate is compelling; whether by introducing two or more BE clients, adding organic IP we already control, or exposure to emerging entities that can catalyze faster and more voluminous market success.

Given the constant and dramatic shifts in healthcare delivery, reimbursement, and paths to market, many young businesses are finding that going it alone is no longer a viable option for commercialization. A seasoned partner like CCI can help emerging entities avoid the typical pitfalls and hurdles that come with building companies in the healthcare sector. While also providing access to a growing network of investors, corporate partners, and subject matter experts, collaboration with CCI leads to fewer costly delays or misdirected drifts that can challenge the viability of the most fragile startups.

Minding the Gaps

The preceding section of this chapter described our assessment instruments that have allowed us to interrogate the innovation infrastructure and the culture of our organization and any other that wishes to engage with us in the contemporary innovation ecosystem. These exercises have provided us with unprecedented insight into the innovation signature of an organization through which we can interpret the personality and promise of future innovation success.

Like its namesake, the global positioning system, the *i*GPS really does simultaneously tell you where you are and where you're going. It has become one of the most important engagement tools in our practice and has allowed us to assist other institutions. The *i*GPS's other parallel to the popular navigation aid is that it's dynamic: the course can be altered to make sure you arrive at your desired destination. When we perform the *i*GPS and discover an institution's innovation assets and liabilities, we can then assist in adjusting the pathway by providing advice or resources. We can amplify operational prowess while identifying discrepancies, redundancies, and deficiencies.

We have identified the five most common gaps, some of which exist in almost any innovation infrastructure or institution:

- **Mission gap.** Discord can develop between innovators dedicated to mission and those entrusted with the financial health of an institution. The most common way we have seen this manifest is when the innovation function reports to the CFO, instead of the CEO or research director. We caution any organization that looks at innovation just as a revenue generator and not as an identity builder and mission server.

- **Infrastructure gap.** In many ways, this is one of the easiest gaps to close. Even when other factors are aligned, there can simply be paucity of professionals familiar with the process of innovation. It's a highly specific engagement that also requires the ability to deal with several factions: innovators, investors, and industry. The two most straightforward ways to remedy this deficiency are to increase institutional investment in recruitment or seek an alliance such as the GHIA.

- **Strategic gap.** This is an internal mismatch within the C-suite when the nonclinical revenue-producing faction and operational leadership cannot agree on the importance of integrating innovation into the overall enterprise direction. In today's terms, an attitude of cutting to prosperity has supplanted a balanced approach to managing assets, including exploiting the potential of IP and relationships derived from it. This must be an internal fix that begins with innovation practitioners demonstrating the multiple benefits that innovation creates.

- **Capital gap.** Successfully funding organic innovation is the most readily recognizable and persistent challenge that all programs face today. The lament from the investment community that what we do can be "too early and too risky" has created a gap between what institutions can fund from their own P&L and what's required to adequately support the growing company.

- **Talent gap.** When mission-driven innovation is successful in bringing an idea to the level of company creation, attracting leadership to take the company to the next stage is critical. The barriers to accomplish this are many, but they may be ameliorated by innovation leadership by maintaining entrepreneur-in-training (EIR) programs or working with internal or external incubators or accelerators.

Once gaps are defined, they can be addressed. Combining the ability to identify areas of potential improvement with the competencies to augment deficiencies is the formula for building a sustainable and successful innovation program.

Partners

Innovation as a Team Sport

The two most critical characteristics of Cleveland Clinic's approach to innovation are process and partnership. The former is objective and demonstrable; the latter can be subjective and ethereal unless pursued with equal discipline.

This chapter describes how Cleveland Clinic engages all innovation stakeholders to optimize the outcomes important to each. Despite healthcare's inherent complexity, basic principles of relationship development and management still are the best way to build sustainable achievement.

You'll read about partnership approaches for rescuing the damaged industry-provider relationship paradigm. We'll also cover ways of honoring the Sunshine Law, while maintaining healthy connection between physicians and corporate vendors. Next, I'll share our perspectives about provider-provider partnerships, which is embodied in Cleveland Clinic's model for collaboration between historical competitors, the Global Healthcare Innovations Alliance (GHIA). I will examine local and statewide economic partnerships that Cleveland Clinic is leading and, finally, partnerships between co-inventors, from individuals to institutions and beyond.

Shifting the Relationship Paradigms

Two relationship structures dominate the supply side of healthcare's economy: vendor-client and competitor. Involvement in mission-driven innovation invites traditional vendors and clients to associate as partners and can turn competitive health systems into collaborators. These are extremely useful relationship configurations at a time when economic pressures resulting from the 2010 U.S. Patient Protection and Affordable Care Act, volume-to-value shifting, and moves to population management are imminent.

Industry-Provider Relationships

There are three doors through which large strategic vendors access healthcare systems: supply chain, direct physician contact, and innovation activity, such as commercial divestment of intellectual property (IP) or codevelopment.

On a given afternoon, we may meet with traditional merchants with whom we're working on technology co-innovation or possibly a divestment. If they have been negotiating with our supply chain (sometimes termed *formulary*) in the morning, they arrive crestfallen. For obvious reasons, hospital systems have been driving hard bargains, especially on physician-choice items. Vendors are hearing that they must participate in an ultracompetitive request-for-proposal (RFP) process after decades of incumbency or that they must meet a specific price for their implants to remain on the shelf.

The innovation function must likewise adapt its expectations and practices. Just as end users—surgeons, for example—are getting more involved in supply-chain decision making by becoming better informed about implant pricing and gaining efficiency by slimming their sets, innovators are also contributing. We're recognizing and rewarding creative game changers that lower cost, democratize care, and improve quality. These initiatives are best pursued with the cooperation of, not at the exclusion of, industry.

Cleveland Clinic encourages (and in some cases, requires) physicians to learn the costs of the equipment, especially the disposables, they utilize during procedures. Quality of care and outcomes are the most important parameters, but exercising fiscal responsibility is another variable that the physician can control.

For example, when Cleveland Clinic's Glickman Urological & Kidney Institute analyzed the differential costs of surgeons performing a common procedure, prostatectomy, the variation was striking. When urologists were made aware of the variation, they convened to analyze everything from the individual cost of sutures to how long each patient remained in the recovery room. The result was a 25 percent reduction in cost. Other institutes have followed suit, addressing costs for cardiac procedures and even liver transplants. Such cost analyses will eventually become standard across our entire enterprise.

These improvements were not made at the expense of industry partners, but in cooperation with them. Care-delivery innovation can take the form of process improvement, but it can also stimulate traditional innovation, inspiring both engaged parties to seek novel technical solutions that remove cost while maintaining quality.

The second portal of industry's historical connection to academic medical centers (AMCs) is direct physician contact. I've discussed the importance of protecting the IP of unsophisticated innovators from going "over the transom" to industry. An additional contraction in the relationship is much more formalized, embodied by the Physician Payments Sunshine Act.

The Sunshine Act was part of the 2010 healthcare law overhaul, and in 2013, the U.S. Centers for Medicare & Medicaid Services released final implementation regulations. At its core, the act requires public reporting of payment and gifts of value made to physicians and teaching hospitals by medical device and pharmaceutical companies. The levels of payment over which reporting is necessary are modest—in the range of $10 for a single event or $100 in annual aggregate.

We unequivocally support this level of transparency. But we also advocate continued exchange between industry and individual physicians to further innovation. If an impregnable barrier is erected between physicians and industry, we'll see stagnation in innovation because we won't understand each other's challenges.

The role of the innovation leader in this emerging situation is chaperone, but not referee. Here are some basic guidelines to manage that relationship and benefit both sides:

- **Monitor conflict of interest (COI).** One of the most important policy contributions that an innovation function can make to the institution is a clear COI policy. Maintaining a contemporary policy that frames the relationships between industry and the provider does not mean that innovation is squelched. Cleveland Clinic has an oft-invoked saying among our leadership: "If there's no interest, there's no conflict." We *want* our caregivers to be sought-after opinion leaders and contributors of new concepts. The key is to manage the conflict by assisting all stakeholders to adhere productively to institutional directives and federal laws.

- **Structure ideation.** How will improvements in existing instruments or drugs happen if there is no discourse between the maker and the prescriber? By the time complications or inferior results are reported in the medical literature, it's far too late to change the course of the product development or manufacturing schedule. The innovation function can solicit unmet needs that each party sees from its unique perspective and conduct forums where co-innovation can take place. This serves to solve problems, protect IP, and provide a steady flow of new ideas to industry, which has reduced its intrinsic research and development capacity, preferring instead to grow by acquisition, not innovation.

- **Educate industry about organic innovation.** I don't blame the large organizations that have elected to grow by acquisition rather than innovation, given the present reduced R&D spend and limited access to physician innovators. To serve shareholders, these companies must diminish risk and maintain profits in the harsh environment of cost repositioning. The way to maintain a positive course out of today's healthcare maelstrom is not cutting to prosperity, but innovating to improvement. It means that industry starts participating in and supporting true early-stage innovation, providing assistance to maintain the development infrastructure that gestates napkin ideas to first-in-man trials. This philosophy represents the cornerstone of the new era in mission-driven innovation.

The innovation function can repair damaged relationships among industry, healthcare systems, and their physicians by embracing philosophies and methodologies that set common goals and engage all parties in partnership.

Provider-Provider Relationships

Over the years, I've asked hundreds of Cleveland Clinic colleagues, "What are the most important innovations that have been contributed by our institution?" Because there is no right answer, I inquire to gain sharper insights about the person and the performance of the innovation function I steward. The answers have typically broken down into two camps: technical and philosophical.

It's certainly no surprise to hear a litany of specific advancements in technique and technology. Everybody at Cleveland Clinic, regardless of specialty, is familiar with the contributions to coronary angiography and bypass grafting. Recent advances, such as the first near-total face transplant, remind us that we continue to be one of the most progressive institutions in the world. This summary is certainly not exhaustive, but it stands as representative of nearly 100 years of creative thinking from a strong, clinically oriented enterprise.

Other colleagues, or sometimes even the same individual, will switch focus and answer the question with our model of care, the influence of our one-year contracting cycles, or the impact of our annual performance reviews. Frankly, most of these can be rolled up under our founding institutional motto, "To act as a unit."

Recently, I've heard a new answer emerge that's a direct result of our innovation strategy: Cleveland Clinic has determined how to *partner* with other institutions. This seemingly inherent or even innocuous statement actually has great complexity and significance.

When our CEO and president, Toby Cosgrove, invited me to return to Cleveland Clinic, he asked what I could contribute to this great institution. I hoped that my surgical practice focused on the care of elite athletes would translate from the Curtis National Hand Center, and, fortunately, it did. But Dr. Cosgrove actually was inquiring about what executive vision I would bring. I said I could help make Cleveland Clinic the "best partner in modern healthcare."

This was not empty rhetoric. Because of extensive experience in professional sports, I know a few things about building championship organizations and fostering team play. Cleveland Clinic was in the unique position to rise above the vicissitudes of hand-to-hand combat with other formidable regional, national, and international competitors and pioneer partnerships between systems of equivalent size and reputation.

Medicine has a long history of relationships between superior and subordinate organizations—the purchase of physician practices or smaller units in strategically located geographies, for example. What I espoused to Dr. Cosgrove was defining a way to create a union of equals, at that time considered almost impossible by most healthcare participants and observers.

Mission-driven innovation is the noncompetitive platform for relationship building between organizations of any size, type, sector, or location. That's a pretty strong statement, so let's back it up with a hypothetical scenario.

Two rival hospital systems, East General and West Memorial, reside in a major metropolitan area. They have a long history of competing for patients, physicians, certificates of need, trainees, and research dollars. Let's assign to East General Hospital a highly evolved technology transfer unit with a reputation for securing patents, executing licenses, and gestating spin-off companies.

Across town at West Memorial, Susan Smith is practicing and innovating at an institution that has not invested in developing an infrastructure for IP commercialization. Dr. Smith is a busy clinician, but she maintains capability and commitment to identifying unmet needs and forwarding solutions. Innovation hasn't been consistently described as part of West Memorial's DNA. Dr. Smith is unaware of her institution's inventor policies, should they even exist, or mechanisms by which ideas can be protected and developed.

The choices for her "napkin ideas" are limited. In frustration, she could file or discard the scribblings that might have led to a disruptive solution to a pressing problem. Or she could share her idea with a vendor, and it will make the all-too-frequent lateral migration to industry without any level of protection or participation by the inventor.

The net result of Dr. Smith's game-changing innovation is that, at best, her hospital can buy it from a vendor in a year or two and get it into her hands to help patients. At worst, nothing happens. No patients will be helped, Dr. Smith is not rewarded, and her hospital gets no funds to further its innovation capability.

Ironically, even East General comes out a loser, as no regional jobs are created by the economic development potential of her concept. If East General and West Memorial could set aside their rivalry when it comes to innovation and collaborate, it becomes a brand-new story.

Let's paint a new picture, now with an alliance between East and West to allow access to state-of-the-art innovation support. Patients' lives are improved and extended by the breakthrough technology or drug Dr. Smith developed. Appropriately, she is financially rewarded, incentivizing additional innovative thinking or possibly investment in growing the technology of others. According to prenegotiated revenue distribution arrangements, both institutions (the inventor's home base and the organization entrusted to develop the technology) benefit. Lastly, jobs are created in the region. If so much advantage can be created when experienced innovation experts assist under-resourced inventors, why would organizations choose myopically to maintain their identities as competitors?

Cleveland Clinic invested millions of dollars and countless hours in developing a core competency in commercial development of IP. We determined that in the area of innovation, partnership outweighed partisanship. So we founded the GHIA, a collaborative network of healthcare systems, academic institutions, and corporate partners from around the world, creating opportunities that benefit patients everywhere through scalable technology development and commercialization.

Realizing Provider Partnership Potential: The Founding of the Global Healthcare Innovations Alliance

Several factors converged to stimulate the foundation of the GHIA, including maturing capability, market demand, and the power of personal connections. But there was also a bit of serendipity.

The invitation for me to return to Cleveland Clinic was unanticipated. My family was very comfortable in Baltimore. MedStar Health was evolving into the largest care-delivery system in the mid-Atlantic. In addition to being chief of the national hand center, I led a systemwide sports medicine entity, MedStar SportsHealth, through which we cared for the Baltimore Ravens, Washington Nationals, and many of the colleges and high schools in the region. In addition, we had launched the Arnold Palmer SportsHealth Center.

I had recently been approached by MedStar's president and CEO, Kenneth A. Samet, about helping to develop a commercialization and corporate venturing entity to be called MedStar Institute for Innovation (MI2). While I didn't stay at MedStar to commence the innovation initiative, my 2010 return to Cleveland to lead Cleveland Clinic Innovations (CCI) allowed me to continue my involvement with MI2.

CCI + MI2 = Start of the GHIA

I knew CCI had enjoyed great success since I departed in 2000. My question was, "How could Cleveland Clinic grow CCI and extend the reach of mission-driven innovation?"

The number of disclosures per year—the currency of innovation on any campus—had leveled off at about 300. This number is astronomical and reflects the extraordinary talent and creativity of Cleveland Clinic colleagues, but the growth curve was nonetheless flat. Unless the staff was expanded by hiring a few prolific innovators or annexing hundreds of creative colleagues in some form of system aggregation, the number of disclosures would likely remain at that level.

Shortly after my homecoming, our team got to work determining whether the CCI process was stable, sustainable, scalable, and transferable. The first two qualifiers are internal checkpoints, while the latter two relate directly to why we founded the GHIA. Stability and sustainability are the basic substrates of a world-class innovation infrastructure. Scalability and transferability define the potential to grow innovation partnership.

Cleveland Clinic was the ideal laboratory for developing an innovation function, owing to the model under which we're all similarly contracted, the high-volume and high-complexity pathologies we treat, and the clinical entrepreneurialism that has pervaded since its inception. Many organizations want what we have: a culture of innovation and a commercialization function that attracts and retains talent, expands creative identity, and generates nonclinical revenue.

But how do you efficiently build and operate an innovation engine in today's environment of austerity? We all recognize that innovation can be nonlinear, at times inefficient and fraught with failure. The nature of innovation collides with the economic realities facing our healthcare leaders, but they also realize the necessity for it as an identity, revenue, recruitment, and patient-care advantage.

The question facing today's hospital system C-suite is not whether innovation should be part of the portfolio, but is the process of joining the innovation fraternity a "buy" or a "build"? Without belaboring the costs of building an innovation entity from scratch, it is hard—rewarding, but hard work. Aside from variables reflected on the balance sheet, the valuable commodity consumed in abundance is time. Top executives dislike delay about as much as ambiguity, and the assembly of a commercialization platform is beset with both.

It would be disingenuous to discourage anyone from chasing this noble pursuit. However, we'd be guilty of withholding a key nugget of advice if we didn't present the contemporary alternative to a homegrown innovation entity—partnering with a going concern.

You've guessed the outcome of the CCI and MI2 story. Because of extraordinary cultural alignment, compelling complementary capabilities, recognition of economies of scale, and the catalytic influence of the personal relationships, we launched the GHIA on January 11, 2011—1.11.11 for all you binary thinkers.

There are those who may think this was easy because our physical separation largely precludes us from competing for patients. No large-scale initiative between healthcare systems is preordained. It takes commitment and trust. These traits were plentiful in Cleveland Clinic's inaugural innovation partnership with MedStar and have remained as we've grown the global alliance. Much of the credit goes to the two CEOs, Toby Cosgrove and Ken Samet, and the tireless champion of innovation at MedStar, physician Mark Smith.

Any alliance is characterized by detailed structures for rights, transactions, governance, and performance standards. The specifics are confidential, but the generalities are relevant.

You identify best individual processes and seek to develop best combined practices. You continuously leverage resources and relationships that are unique to the members because of region or are attracted by your collective scale.

We Complete the "Innovation Triangle" and Then Double It

Through a combination of strategic outreach and fielding of inquiries from CEOs around the country who quickly learned of our model, we've rapidly grown the GHIA. The "innovation triangle" was completed within a year of the MedStar transaction when Northwell Health (formerly North Shore-LIJ Health System) joined us. Again, the personal and professional cohesiveness between Dr. Cosgrove and Northwell Health president and CEO Michael J. Dowling played a part. Having an innovation evangelist like Kevin J. Tracey, a talented neurosurgeon and world-class researcher who runs the Feinstein Institute for Medical Research, facilitated the alliance.

Once three of the biggest healthcare systems in the country showed that they could form a consortium to further medical innovation, the proverbial match was thrown into the gasoline shed. The benefits of scale economies, co-innovation, shared insight, and resource supplementation started to fuel growth. Three esteemed partners joined nearly simultaneously in 2012: ProMedica Health System, The Innovation Institute at St. Joseph Health, and University of Notre Dame.

ProMedica may have created more local buzz because it is a $2 billion progressive healthcare system based in Toledo, Ohio, only 120 miles from Cleveland. The scenario of regional rivals described earlier was tested in reality, with the result being enhanced cooperation to serve the citizens of our state and around the world.

The Innovation Institute didn't just take the GHIA west of the Rocky Mountains; it brought in very progressive thinking about monetizing the core services of large hospital systems and keen financial modeling capabilities.

When Notre Dame joined us, it caused a modicum of confusion for some observers, but it is completely consistent with our model to network culturally aligned organizations with supplementary and complementary capabilities. Notre Dame brought to the GHIA a world-class biomedical engineering program and progressive business and law schools. If our country is to maintain primacy in innovation, all members of the ecosystem must be introduced to the inner workings as early and expertly as possible. Notre Dame's inclusion also brought to the fore the issue of recognizing and rewarding scholars for participation in advancing ideas that have both scientific and commercial applications.

Commercial Innovators Come on Board

Innovation occurs at the intersection of knowledge domains. We knew that restricting membership to AMCs and research universities would be limiting.

Our prerequisite for corporate partners is that they seek to transform healthcare by leveraging special skills, resources, and relationships. The initial entry was motion-control giant Parker Hannifin Corp. If it moves, Parker's products control or touch it. The Parker relationship taught the global alliance how to work with organizations that weren't exactly like us.

One of the links that accelerated the partnership's success was Parker's annual Best Mousetrap competition, which showcases evolving projects in many of its manufacturing divisions. Since we've engaged in this "beauty contest" of Parker's coolest technologies, every year 5 to 10 new concepts have been brought to the GHIA. Several promising technologies have been submitted for regulatory approval in the United States and Europe, with commercial launch anticipated by early 2016. Two are devices, an optically clear endoscopic sheath designed to minimize risk of infection during surgery and a side-entry torquing device used to direct intravascular guidewires.

In the ensuing years, we've added chemicals and materials leader the Lubrizol Corporation to the GHIA for the unique capabilities in the company's expanding Life Sciences division, and Cox Enterprises, Inc., a communications and media titan. It was again difficult for some to initially see why a cable company and a hospital system should partner. The Cox forte is connecting people; the company touches one in three Americans every day. We can think of no better partner to help medicine move toward mobile platforms and into the home than one of the world leaders in bringing information to people.

The National Aeronautics and Space Administration (NASA) is our newest GHIA partner. NASA will share priceless insights about novel materials, remote monitoring, fluid and gas handling in harsh environments, and equipment miniaturization. The design challenges faced by NASA are surprisingly similar to those hospitals tackle when equipping an operating room.

These partnerships demonstrate the breadth of mission-driven innovation. Opening the aperture to different perspectives and skills, even those heretofore not considered relevant to healthcare delivery, strengthens our capabilities to serve patients.

Optimizing the Alliance

In every sport, there are both responsibilities and rewards attached to managing the all-star team. Likewise, there are expectations in harnessing the talent and capability residing in the best and brightest specialty practitioners.

The alliance has a North Star: the benefit of patients. All partners seek to develop and deploy best-practice models and collaborate to accelerate the pace and maximize the efficiency of medical innovation to benefit patients.

For example, Maryland physical therapists Jodi Maron Barth and Gincy Lockhart Stezar came up with a way to accelerate the rehabilitation of patients suffering from partial facial paralysis resulting from Bell's palsy, Ramsay Hunt syndrome, Lyme disease, acoustic neuroma, or stroke.

Using only duct tape, cardboard, and mirrors, these co-inventors built prototypes to replicate and produce a symmetrical image of the nonaffected side of the face. They then deployed Hebbian learning theories[1] that had helped amputees improve function. Their paralysis patients demonstrated measurable improvement and elevated self-esteem.

Through their affiliation with GHIA partner MedStar Health, Barth and Stezar leveraged commercialization advice from Stephen Kinsey of CCI. He helped the inventors hire a developer and bring to market the iPad app Face2Face Facial Palsy. Barth and Stezar formed the Center for Facial Recovery™ in 2014 and are now helping patients worldwide.

The app is available in the Apple Store and through ADEO, the GHIA's e-commerce spin-off that sells digital healthcare products developed by alliance partners directly to hospitals, private-practice physicians, and patients. Along with mobile apps, inventory includes more than a dozen survey tools, playbooks, and software solutions. In addition to Face2Face Facial Palsy, there's a fall-risk assessment tool for cancer patients and a hearing protection app that monitors ambient noise levels. Cologene, the hereditary-disease-management software, is offered in ADEO as well. Most items are available for immediate download, and ADEO also offers infrastructure and teams to help configure products and services into a client's workflow.

The GHIA is not a series of bilateral relationships but a network of high-performing institutions that can work independently, as focused subsets, or as a singular juggernaut of creativity. Relationships are governed by equitably constructed joint management agreements. The environment of trust fosters co-innovation.

As the alliance has matured, we see greater opportunities and expressions of strategic innovation. There may be no better prepared think tank for tackling the most complex and pressing problems facing global healthcare than our consortium. Yes, we have plenty of primary initiatives to pursue, but entities like corporations, foundations, and governments can bring their challenges to the GHIA as a one-stop shop for everything from creative solutions to validation.

The formation of our alliance has accelerated development of a distributed competency across all the partner organizations. The organization with more resources or experience in selected domains provides that service or takes the lead. Moreover, we can exercise the additive power of co-innovation, as often we find the lock on one campus meets a key on another.

The most compelling benefit of establishing an association of this type is portfolio building. The direct result of associating institutions of prolific creativity is the opportunity to aggregate the largest collection of IP in healthcare. The benefit is to explore more of a portfolio approach to its management.

As traditional nonprofit institutions continue to struggle in funding research and innovation activities, not only does investigating ways to extract value from IP become relevant and attractive, but novel funding concepts also should be studied. The GHIA has taken on this responsibility, innovating around models to fund the practice of putting ideas to work.

Our consortium has been examining sophisticated financial engineering concepts including the securitization of IP, which could be game changing to the way we support future creative pursuits. It seems only natural that we would extend the spirit of innovation to all aspects of the engagement, including ways to make the pursuit sustainable from an economic perspective.

While alliance partners were approaching this in a more rudimentary fashion by cobbling together funding from the institutions and government to fuel the innovation function, essentially working from a micro basis, Andrew W. Lo of the MIT Sloan School of Management was exploring securitization on the mega level.[2] He is proposing a multibillion-dollar fund to bring substantial resources to the problems facing early-stage research.

Economic Development Partnership in Our Own Backyard

Cleveland Clinic is the largest employer in the history of northeast Ohio and the largest employer in Cleveland, with more than 43,000 caregivers. The second spot is occupied by University Hospitals Health System at about half that number. Healthcare is the economic driver of our region. CCI has placed community economic development among our priorities. We partnered with the Fairfax Renaissance Development Corporation, a nonprofit whose mission is to strengthen neighborhoods in northeastern Ohio through comprehensive community development, in building a 50,000-square-foot, $23 million incubator. It houses CCI's offices and is the headquarters of the Global Cardiovascular Innovation Center (GCIC), a collaborative of six Ohio-based AMCs and research universities that is acquiring, incubating, and commercializing technologies. The companies that we have gestated there have created nearly 1,500 jobs in our city.

A compelling economic reality is that the only net new-job creators in our country over the past two decades are new companies less than five years old. Healthcare-related businesses are at the center of this new market. These facts point to the critical role medical-innovation-derived startups play in fueling our growth.

Several companies that provide our nascent entities with services such as prototyping have been attracted to join the incubator. We have a second site just blocks away already staked out for a sister building. Our dream is to dot the periphery of Cleveland Clinic's campus with these beacons of innovation, then fill in around them with residential, retail, dining, and entertainment destinations.

Extending beyond Cleveland, in 2013, a Cleveland Clinic–led consortium of Ohio AMCs and research universities was awarded one of three National Institutes of Health Centers for Accelerated Innovations grants to improve translation of basic science into commercially viable products that improve patient care and advance public health. Our center includes Case Western Reserve University, Ohio State University, University of Cincinnati, and Cincinnati Children's Hospital Medical Center in a seven-year program during which time nearly $13 million will be deployed to promote commercialization of discovery science targeting heart, lung, blood, and sleep disorders and diseases.

Partnership Between Inventors

The creative potential of different-size groups and their constitutions is explored through the lens of what we have observed in the two decades of operation of CCI. Because various engagements may require different approaches, there is no-one-size-fits-all answer, but here's what we've seen work and ways innovation output may be enhanced by optimizing the creative team.

- **Lone wolf.** While history is replete with the likes of Archimedes, Leonardo da Vinci, Sir Isaac Newton, and Benjamin Franklin, the single inventor—or lone wolf—model of invention is simply not as prevalent in CCI's pool of disclosures. Between two-thirds and three-quarters of invention disclosures are submitted by more than one person. Even the times when a single inventor has enjoyed success, there is usually acknowledgment of a close cadre of advisors and facilitators or a team of supporters. The lone wolf model exists and is OK if your name is Einstein, but we don't count on this being the dominant source of IP flow.

- **Dynamic duo.** We've observed a curious phenomenon over the years building and operating an innovation function concerning the potency of two minds melding as one. It's impossible to say that two can be the magic number, but whether it's Watson and Crick or Lennon and McCartney, there does seem to be something special about the power of two. My guess is that it may be the optimal way to combine complementarity, parsimony, and dynamic tension. Keeping it to two also doesn't hurt the other important innovation variable, speed.

- **Relay race.** We have seen organizations and some smaller teams attempt to engage in sequential innovation, whereby a subset of individuals takes a project as far as they can, then passes it off to another group. We believe this model to be ineffective; whether it's thought to take advantage of specific expertise or minimize biased thinking, we're just not fans. Most modern innovation infrastructures provide for more interaction, not less, as ideas develop. That isn't to say that expertise activated at the right time isn't valuable. We simply advocate for the innovation team to spend as much of the journey together as possible to maximize the outcome, instead of artificially shielding potentially important contributors from key stages of development.

- **Innovation ecosystem.** It should come as no surprise that we would identify the network approach as the highest aspirational level. After first uniting the individual with the institution over its IP estate, and then combining an alliance of high-performing entities, the next step is making the entire machinery of innovation hum by managing it as a single organism. We find ways to simultaneously grow and balance a larger consortium. This pursuit will be enabled by evolving technologies in big data and the realization of the economic and social climate around healthcare. One day, we may wake up and say that we can't grow the GHIA any bigger, but that would result only from an inability to render service and leadership to all partners according to what they need and deserve.

Innovation can and will happen by almost any partnership permutation imaginable. The more the leadership understands about its dynamics, the better the process and its eventual outcome. Setting the stage for optimal interaction with a variety of partners and deployment of resources at critical times is one of the key challenges and responsibilities of today's innovation practitioner.

Place

Building a Home for Innovation:
From Incubators to Constellations

If we're to view innovation as a tangible discipline, we need a home for it. The concept is not new. But environment is increasingly recognized as an innovation enabler. Whether it's a lab, incubator, or cluster, a sense of place and its accompanying resources are a key contributor to innovation success.

Considerations regarding the optimal innovation environment are somewhat contradictory: Structure a space that's informal and unstructured. Have technology at the fingertips of the innovator, but make sure it's unobtrusive. Build places that foster direct connection and trust, yet can access outside expertise immediately.

Cleveland Clinic has been the convener, architect, landlord, and tenant in practically every physical manifestation known to the innovation ecosystem. This chapter will visit all the addresses of innovation—the buildings, neighborhoods, and broader geographies—and share our lessons learned.

Place is important because innovation occurs optimally at the intersection of knowledge domains. Throughout history, the greatest scholarly advances, technical breakthroughs, and artistic developments occurred in the port cities of the world, where people of different cultures convened and shared fresh ideas. For example, Florence was the epicenter of the Renaissance largely because the Medicis made it a magnet for merchants, artisans, philosophers, architects, scientists, and musicians.[1]

I subscribe to the law of propinquity, which means nearness in place or time, amplified by an intimate intellectual connection. Propinquity differs from simple geographic closeness because the term implies physical proximity *and* cultural alignment, two critical variables for a great personal relationship, professional partnership, or creative collaboration. Propinquity can accelerate innovation victories and increase their value.

Our job as innovation leaders is to foster propinquity—to network creative people, new ideas, and necessary resources to maximize opportunities and the likelihood of success. Cleveland Clinic, as one of the world's iconic medical systems, has the gravitational pull to attract colleagues with prodigious talent and big ideas. So our focus is on resource allocation and process management in an environment ideally suited for innovation.

Incubators as the Front Door of Innovation

If innovation means putting ideas to work, where does innovation clock in? Where is the front door, or more important for commercialization, the loading dock or sales counter? Where do ideas become innovations and, eventually, entrepreneurial companies? The answer for the past several decades is the incubator.

When Cleveland Clinic pioneered having an innovation function within a nonprofit hospital environment, we recognized there might be limitations to how far an idea could be taken toward commercialization on our campus. We weren't going to build a medical device fabricating plant next to our operating rooms. However, there are advantages to both the institution and the fledgling company of close proximity during the most vulnerable time of development, incubation.

This section of the chapter will: (1) define the contemporary incubator and compare incubation models; (2) describe how Cleveland Clinic Innovations (CCI) leveraged physical space to promote core competency in innovation and successfully spun off several companies; and (3) equip the reader to advocate for a dedicated physical space for innovation.

Incubation Models

Incubation essentially means optimizing the chances of success for an entity that needs to transition from a less mature to a more mature state. It requires a catalytic environment that facilitates resource access. The energy that activates the catalysis is collaboration, which is influenced by proximity.

An incubator is the cradle of innovation and should be a dedicated space that fosters creativity and collaboration. An incubator should house services facilitating the growth of commercially viable entities and provide one-stop shopping to outside stakeholders.

You must identify the specific advantages an incubator may impart if you're to sell the concept of building a physical space and eventually optimize innovation in it at your institution.

At Cleveland Clinic, we had the opportunity to create a novel incubator model to support promising ideas at their most vulnerable stages. We continue to improve upon this critical link between organic institutional innovation and industry's commercial development.

In the mid-1990s, when Joseph F. Hahn, chairman of the Division of Surgery, and I were scouring Cleveland Clinic for resources to pilot my original orthopaedic device portfolio through the internal technology-transfer process that would become CCI, we found the exercise time-consuming and sometimes frustrating. CCI's present location had not yet been conceived, so this exercise required visits to both on- and off-campus legal offices, a variety of engineering facilities, and a small prototyping lab.

We were not only motivated to develop a sustainable process to control IP, we were also interested in aggregating the resources in one place to introduce efficiency and facilitate the engagement for the busy inventor whose main priority was the clinic, operating room, or laboratory. After I left Cleveland for Baltimore in 2000, Dr. Hahn and Chris Coburn, CCI's inaugural executive director, were successful in securing a former dialysis area as CCI's original home. This was one of the first prototypes for the modern incubator, now prevalent in both the nonprofit and for-profit sectors.

I admit to usually using the terms *incubator* and *accelerator* almost interchangeably or in some form of hyphenated mash-up. Any physical location (or even virtual network) that reduces risk, lowers barriers, accelerates knowledge transfer, and increases commercial opportunity deserves both mantles. Cleveland Clinic has enjoyed more success with a model lighter on nomenclature but heavier on discipline at the front of the technology-development process and operated in a flexible fashion later in the commercial maturity cycle to customize resources to needs.

When does an incubator become an accelerator and then a launching pad? The reason most of us in the mission-driven innovation sphere eschew those labels is because our entities typically have characteristics of both, and we don't usually pass off companies at predetermined development milestones. The distinction is not as important as thoughtful operation on behalf of evolving companies.

Both the incubator and the accelerator deal with early-stage companies—again, probably one of the most confusing terms in healthcare innovation. To some, early stage means prerevenue, while others believe that companies already grossing millions still deserve this moniker. When your early stage is often scribbled on the back of a napkin, you have a slightly different view of the entire continuum! The labels don't matter; the protection and resourcing do.

There isn't much dispute about the incubator being where most organic innovations land when they move from idea to proof of concept and definition by initial funding and leadership. If the incubator does its job, the innovator evolves into a nascent business builder surrounded by many of the resources that he or she may not have even known were necessary. Furthermore, once in an incubator, the innovator is surrounded by like-minded, enthusiastic, and equally immature colleagues going through the same growing pains.

By the time the concept emerges from CCI's internal process, we have performed so much due diligence through analysis of technical and clinical merit and market feasibility that calling the invention's next station an incubator seems disingenuous. This is true for most innovation functions starting with ideas delivered to them by experts who have identified an unmet need. Yet we still appreciate that there is a long way to go and want to "grease the gears."

Our physical incubator, the Global Cardiovascular Innovation Center (the GCIC building) houses 20 to 25 emerging companies and several service providers attracted by the dynamic environment where their special skills can be utilized by a number of fledgling companies. The first floor is occupied by CCI's administrative function, so we maintain constant contact with our gestating entities. Most important, we sit at the periphery of Cleveland Clinic's main campus because the most valuable asset of any of our portfolio companies is access to the primary innovation engine that is Cleveland Clinic.

The next stop for survivors of whatever process you consider incubation is the accelerator. If the incubator is where seeds and soil are mixed and initially exposed to sunlight, the accelerator is the hothouse where growing conditions are optimized through structure. The emerging business is surrounded by the elements of the commercial ecosystem in which it will be immersed throughout the rest of its market run.

Besides the obvious catalytic activity taking place there, the reason why the term *accelerator* is applicable is the velocity of almost every part of the entrepreneur's engagement. It's like drinking from a fire hose. Within the accelerator model, the validity of the company is pressure-tested by potential investors. The clock is usually ticking at the traditional accelerator; whether it's weeks, months, or as much as a year, the heat is on, allowing the business to either catch fire or flame out.

Both incubators and accelerators are where innovation grows up to be entrepreneurship. The commonality of infrastructure, mentorship, access, and validation far outweighs whatever subtle differences may exist between routes of entry or time periods during which a company can remain in the ecosystem.

CCI's successful approach to the continuum of commercialization-incubation-acceleration and the importance of place are illustrated by Cleveland HeartLab, Inc. (CHL). It's a fast-growing spin-off company with a niche in detection of heart attack and stroke-related biomarkers, developed by researcher and inventor Stanley L. Hazen. CHL first inhabited the CCI building. Initially, the eight employees were comfortable, but the volume of tests eventually stressed the space. Cramped conditions and wooing by attractive out-of-town investors led CHL to consider leaving Cleveland. But proximity to Cleveland Clinic, availability of favorable rents and support services, and a tax credit from the State of Ohio for job creation kept CHL here. It rapidly grew to more than 80 employees after moving from 7,000 square feet in CCI's building to 27,000 square feet in nearby MidTown Tech Park. CHL continues to grow a few blocks from Cleveland Clinic and consistently seeks to expand its portfolio of tests by licensing novel assays developed in our laboratories.

The space and services CCI provides to spin-off companies is vital, but there comes a day when their growth outpaces our ability to nurture them adequately. Maintaining a currency with real estate locations and having access to state funding sources gives CCI an advantage that translates into success for the companies, our institution, and the region.

Does a nurturing incubator increase the likelihood of evolving concepts that are successfully translated into commercial concerns? Contrary to common sense or basic deductive reasoning, the answer appears to be no, if you believe much of the scholarly data and business media. It's estimated that 90 percent of these instruments will fail—not 90 percent of gestating companies, but 90 percent of the incubators and accelerators themselves.[2]

Here's where one of the fundamental differences between for-profit thinking about innovation incubators/accelerators and the mission-driven approach becomes obvious. These commercial incubator failures are determined by return on the investments made to start them. The reasons for failure of the incubators and/or the companies they are gestating are the usual suspects that plague each startup: lack of funding, mentorship, and business development connectivity to key transactional resources (financiers, clients, investment bankers, and potential acquirers). Aside from the thrill of gaining admission to a prestigious accelerator program or of participating in beauty contests with investors, there may be little appeal for the best-in-class ideas to relinquish the customary 7 percent of equity demanded by the typical commercial accelerator.

The philosophy and operation of the mission-driven incubator-accelerator is fundamentally different. While the following list of characteristics is likely incomplete, it highlights the divergence in model from the commercial entity:

- **Admission.** Mission-driven projects come through the institutional pipeline, versus an open, public competitive admissions process. They emanate from a domain expert who recognizes an unmet need and solves it right on your campus. Then the concept is exposed to the rigorous processes within the innovation function that is likewise controlled by the institution.

- **Timing.** Most mission-driven models don't have strict limits or cycles that create artificial time pressures to succeed or fail. Academic medical centers (AMCs), specifically, are in it for the long haul because what we're developing may change lives or the way we deliver care to large populations. Starting a stopwatch on innovation, as many commercial incubators are forced to do, isn't aligned with the basic tenets of mission-driven innovation.

- **Service.** The mission-driven incubator-accelerator maintains a similar type and amount of physical services and human resources as a commercial entity, but benefits from economies of scale through affiliation with a major institution. Our incubator is an extension of our institution and enjoys every advantage from proximity, resource sharing, and access—these are huge advantages that have fueled our success.

- **Equity position.** Most AMC and research university IP policies call for an equity position to be shared between the inventor and the institution from the outset of idea generation and development. However, Cleveland Clinic's model and that of the Global Healthcare Innovations Alliance (GHIA) includes no additional equity stake simply for housing in the sponsored incubator-accelerator. Removing an economic disincentive is beneficial enough, but it also frees up capital to be recirculated into the core business.

- **Connectivity and cross-pollination.** The sense of community that exists when entrepreneurs grow up together is motivating and nourishing. That isn't the sole purview of mission-driven incubators, but it is unique on AMC and research university campuses. The reason is that these innovators also practice together or share a research focus and feel loyalty to the sponsor institution. There is freedom to share ideas and resources. Undoubtedly, this is why incubators and accelerators in proximity to the academic center often thrive.

We are focused on service and connectivity to our teeming main campus, but we have always been light on meddling in the daily affairs and operations of our spin-offs. We hold board seats and are always available at critical navigation milestones—for example, introducing companies to potential clients.

But don't mistake proximity for obtrusiveness. Walking the line between active assistance and intrusive interference is a tightrope almost every mission-driven innovation engine will face in starting an incubator. It has taken time and experience, but CCI has done this expertly and shares that knowledge freely with other organizations.

We have confidence in the quality of our ideas, the rigor of our basic innovation infrastructure vetting the technologies, and the nurturing environment our incubator provides. Some may consider the approach we take as our portfolio companies mature to be passive, like "latchkey parents"; we just think it's practical. Let entrepreneurs do what they do best and allow the market forces to work with minimal interference.

Selling the Incubator Concept

Let's start with why it might be logical for an institution to contemplate creating a physical space to serve as the nucleus for innovation and entrepreneurial activity. The sole focus of the incubator is to accelerate and facilitate the commercialization of transcendent ideas; most argue that this takes place through colocation or clustering.

Reputation and resources are at stake when entertaining a decision of this magnitude, so innovation leaders must be prepared to sell the value of the incubator concept. Have both subjective and objective data at your fingertips.

The decision is informed by multiple variables, ranging from depth of talent and idea flow to financial resources. To take some pressure off the front end of the process, remind all participants that a decision against investing in a physical plant doesn't have be considered permanent; staggered or near-simultaneous planning can always take place while an incubator is being launched programmatically. We caution that this decision can't always follow the normal formula of *incremental revenue:incremental spend*. The return on innovation investment takes a while to develop, and often the pump needs to be primed.

It may make sense to concentrate on an institutional strength to accelerate the idea flow and potential success. Your organization may be heavy into health information technology (HIT) or medical devices. An anchor strategy makes the argument more compelling and informs the type of physical space required. Don't disregard the possibilities that arise from juxtaposing neighbors of different backgrounds, but cross-fertilization potential is maximized when tenants are at least remotely related.

Unlike other decisions that the CEO, CFO, and trustees may be accustomed to making based upon P&L statements or business plans (aside from possible real estate management elements inherent to incubators), this decision is more a vote of confidence. The innovation champion must bring passion and optimism and be prepared for pushback, especially in organizations still grappling with how to budget innovation.

This is especially true in the early years of programs when revenues are episodic or nonexistent, but there are always going to be dry spells in this business. In fact, when it seems that creativity is at a nadir is the time when something catalytic like an incubator may have the most impact.

What Should the Incubator Have to Serve
Your Clients and Their Clients?

The aim of the incubator is to aggregate what will help the innovator become an entrepreneur, removing distractions and time sinks associated with foraging for necessary resources and relationships.

Technical or operational infrastructure comes first. The checklist typically includes wet labs, a wired environment, and computing capabilities. Modular walls or flexible interior design elements, like furniture on wheels, can maximize attractiveness to a variety of different companies and minimize the hassles as companies grow.

Full-time, skilled IT professionals are a necessity. The incubator sponsor cannot cut corners in this area. Having skilled IT professionals is one of the most critical contributors to a fledgling company's success, but they can be hard to find and expensive to hire, which is why they are such a logical resource to be shared by tenants. Despite the advanced knowledge Millennials all appear to have with the digital economy, dedicated IT resources will be welcome. There's likely the need for Health Insurance Portability and Accountability Act (HIPAA)–compliant servers if you're hosting healthcare and informatics companies.

Don't forget about parking. You're building an environment in which emerging companies are going to do business. Adding to the young companies' professional identity and servicing them to recruit talent and entertain clients means maintaining the expected amenities, like parking. Only slightly less appreciated is nearby food service, a full kitchen, and a communal break room that can promote cross-pollination between tenants.

At CCI, we have food trucks come in once or twice a week—what a hit! This not only nourishes the bodies and minds of the innovators, but also adds to the contemporary vibe of the incubator environment.

It also never hurts to have a fishbowl, an informal communal space, replete with seating and equipment conducive to stimulating and capturing stream-of-consciousness thinking. The fishbowl is the contemporary water cooler around which innovators from different entities convene to compare notes and potentially create the electricity that solves existing problems or identifies future directions. Having the type of wall coverings on which innovators can write and draw and then capture their scribblings with their smartphones replaces the conventional napkin.

A bull pen of talent that can be distributed and democratized makes for an attractive incubator. Ready access to the expertise and experience of seasoned veterans may be the greatest asset incubators provide. CCI has approached this need in two ways. The entire staff, including the chief innovation officer, resides right in our incubator, so the people who helped the companies through their fledgling stage remain close by as companies mature. In addition, we have entrepreneurs-in-residence (EIRs) who can provide ready insights on navigating the path toward the marketplace.

It's not uncommon for the EIRs to transition into more permanent roles in management or governance within the companies they mentor. The pool of EIRs is designed to be frequently refreshed; as serial entrepreneurs exit successful companies, they often have time and energy to devote to protégés. Creating these win-win scenarios is one of the more compelling arguments for maintaining an incubator structure.

Our EIR program seeks to maintain a mix of domain expertise, career stages, and geographic distribution. Most of CCI's EIRs, like physicians, have a general knowledge of emerging innovations across the spectrum of healthcare but concentrate on a specialty area. Company building in medical devices, therapeutics and diagnostics, and HIT can present different challenges and require specific insights, so we maintain a stable of EIRs who represent these key domains. Regarding career stages, balance the seasoned, serial impresario with the enthusiastic early-career entrepreneur who may have just completed a second or third exit.

There is a regional or cluster mentality that still seems to exist in the innovation ecosystem, despite free information exchange across state or international boundaries. Building a mosaic of EIR talent with a wider geographic perspective may have benefits, as the EIRs can relate what is happening in other areas of the country. Ensuring that EIRs have the chance to interact can be a confidence builder and catalyst for success for your incubator companies.

One of the most logical and engaged sources of EIRs are the incubator alumni. They have walked a mile in the shoes of the tenants and crossed the finish line. The graduates have the experience, but it's multiplied by their enthusiasm for the incubator concept. Keep the successful entrepreneurs spawned through your process relevant and involved as mentors.

We also leverage the strength of our institutional identity to assemble the appropriate technical and financial players. Networking is slightly different in the healthcare innovator/ entrepreneur community than in the business sector. We tend to bring investors, potential clients, and acquirers to the incubating companies—they are visiting Cleveland Clinic anyway, conducting supplier-client business. That isn't to say we haven't mounted more than our share of road shows. Those who desire a sneak peek into tomorrow's solutions and promising investments are attracted to the incubator because it's an efficient way to be immersed. Connect with those who administer your supply chain (also called *formulary*) to bring visitors.

The final recommendation is a communications function. The incubator should be a source of pride for the parent institution or sponsor, as well as all other emerging companies that reside within. Company milestones, especially key investment rounds, product launches, and exits, should be very public. Parent institutions, which usually maintain a robust marketing and public relations capability, can teach the young companies about getting their messages out.

What Are the Incubator's Mission, Vision, and Goals?

Never underestimate the importance of defining mission and vision, nor the difficulties encountered in doing so. We don't stray from CCI's core mission: serving inventors and entrepreneurs by assisting them to develop innovations focused on improving and extending human life. How is that expressed in the operation of our incubator?

When we developed our incubator-accelerator, it focused on support, access, and validation for innovative Cleveland Clinic colleagues and those of our GHIA partners. By combining the home office of CCI with the incubator function, there's bilateral benefit: those engaged in organic innovation are motivated by seeing colleagues in the throes of company creation, and emerging enterprises have access to a steady stream of new ideas and talented individuals.

Enhanced institutional identity, community economic development, and talent attraction are consequences of executing to our mission. Innovation success is self-perpetuating, as graduates become mentors, investors, and serial entrepreneurs.

How Will the Incubator's Success Be Measured?

Cleveland Clinic's measures of success reflect more than occupancy and company performance and include innovator service, identity advancement, and community partnership. Operation of an incubator should at minimum be budget-neutral. Some universities and hospital systems have been very successful at managing the incubator as a revenue-producing real estate asset. However, the yardstick by which the innovation community gauges an incubator's success is the attainments of its companies.

Some common metrics to consider are:

- Number of tenant companies and how many were grown organically versus attracted from outside the institution

- Number of new business starts generated from the incubator's sponsor institution

- Amount of follow-on investment attracted by incubator companies

- Whether the incubator has attracted support companies, meaning platform technologies or service providers drawn by the opportunity to interact with gestating companies

- Number of jobs created, the holy grail for economic development and elected officials

- Velocity of product/business development once a company becomes an incubator tenant

- Quantified usage patterns of shared incubator services and expansion/contraction activity of tenants

- Number and success of ideas/companies that were created by interactions among incubator companies

- Amount of private-sector funding, governmental grants, or philanthropic donations and how the deployment of these monies has been transformative for the incubator and companies

- Graduation rates, recognizing that optimal company size and timing of exit or acquisition are variables that cannot be controlled by the landlord

While we consider the accomplishments of an incubator company in the larger marketplace to be relevant, it can be a somewhat artificial reflection of the incubator's success. Anecdotes of achievement are motivating for the sponsor and the other tenants, but we refrain from counting the lofty statistics generated by big winners as singular incubator triumphs. That line of thinking would identify the garages of Bill Gates and Steve Jobs as the world's foremost incubators.

What's the End Game: When Does a Startup Exit the Incubator?

It can be challenging to decide when a startup no longer needs the nurturing environment of the incubator-accelerator. Many incubator programs have prescribed cycles of engagement, but CCI has never maintained that rigid structure. Instead, we work with startups to recognize the time when the accelerator can become a launching pad. The variables that inform us typically include:

- Size and growth trajectory of the firm relative to available physical space

- Funding cycle and perceived need for support from the institution or incubator staff in raising more capital

- Regional availability of affordable office space that supports the needs of emerging enterprises

- Stability and quality of the startup's leadership and governance

- Intimacy needed with the sponsor institution—clinical trials, biomedical engineering, or medicinal chemistry expertise, for example

These are just some considerations for determining when a startup is ready to exit. We have never kicked anybody out; all exits have been logical decisions made by systematically monitoring key indicators, augmented by our gut feelings. It never fails—when one young startup flies the nest, there's another coming in to take its place. Our incubator has been full since it opened in 2010, and we've completed plans for a second building merely blocks away.

What Can an Incubator Do for Local Economic Development?

Aside from the job creation that may accompany the physical construction of a building, incubators have unique potential for enhancing their local economies. Community economic development comes from growth of a regional innovation cluster and strengthened ties between the academic and business communities.

We are very proud that our incubator, the GCIC, was partnered with the Fairfax Renaissance Development Corporation (FRDC) from the outset. The FRDC is a nonprofit community development entity dedicated to new construction, housing rehabilitation, and community safety programs. It was a perfect fit to bridge the growing Cleveland Clinic footprint with an important historical neighborhood and its own economic development mission.

An innovation cluster benefits local economies by providing optimal environments for developing companies employing talented individuals. Typically, these are high wage earners, which translates into an increased tax base. The downstream spending by these recruits has obvious influence. The effect is multiplied when the fledgling companies finally spin off. Granted, some will follow investment dollars or seek special geographies that facilitate their next steps. However, the majority of companies will remain in the area where they were hatched.

Fostering more intimate relationships with the business community has multiple positive effects, including opportunities for cross-pollination of ideas and strategic investment. A secondary benefit for industry partners is the early targeting of talent and acquisition targets.

To date, CCI and its incubator have accounted for approximately 1,500 jobs. There are a number of indirect jobs accruing from the spin-offs themselves and the additional service providers that support them. We think this cycle of growth is just getting started.

A Cluster-to-Constellation Strategy, with Cleveland Clinic at the Core

It's been a quarter-century since Michael Porter put forward the concept of the regional innovation cluster, the geographic concentration of interconnected resources focused upon advancement in a selected domain.[3]

Regional innovation clusters arise from core competencies and concentrated knowledge and resources. It's logical that advanced ideas and improved processes would grow in such a cauldron. Potential participants and consumers alike are magnetically drawn to the maturing hub to fulfill needs and aspirations. Northeastern Ohio has become a cluster for medical innovation, with Cleveland Clinic as the nucleus.

What's fueling this growth? Those desiring to practice medicine in a stimulating, collegial, and innovative environment are drawn like moths to a flame.

The center of the medical universe has always been where the patient and doctor meet—that's why you can reach the pinnacle of your craft in places such as Cleveland or Rochester, Minnesota, home of Mayo Clinic. If you want to make movies, you need to be in Los Angeles. If you want to create wine, Napa Valley. But if you want to move the needle in healthcare, Cleveland is the place for you.

The economic impact is profound. Cuyahoga County, in which Cleveland resides, has the sixth-highest U.S. healthcare-related employment census and ranks third in job growth among the top hospital employment cities. Healthcare worker income increased by over $1 billion in the period 2000–2011.[4] Cleveland Clinic alone accounts for nearly $13 billion of economic impact to the city and surrounding Northeastern Ohio region.[5]

Recalling that we're emphasizing the value of place on innovation identity, two specific places warrant mention in our cluster discussion. First is the Cleveland Health-Tech Corridor, a three-mile swath east of downtown where biomedical, healthcare, and technology companies find close proximity to four leading healthcare institutions, four academic centers, and more than 130 high-tech and health-tech companies engaged in the business of innovation.

Along with Cleveland Clinic, you'll find Case Western Reserve University, Cleveland State University, and University Hospitals Health System. The Greater Cleveland Regional Transit Authority's HealthLine transit system moves patients and caregivers alike throughout this medical and innovation hub. Health-Tech partners have struck a harmonious balance between competition and collaboration. When it comes to advancing innovation, we're on the same team.

The area is attractive to startups because of favorable rent, availability of support services, and proximity to institutions from which the fledgling companies emanated or to whom they are trying to sell.

The other noteworthy place anchoring Cleveland's healthcare innovation cluster is the new Global Center for Health Innovation (GCHI). Part of an ambitious half-billion-dollar project that brought the city a world-class, 750,000-square-foot convention center, the "Globe" was initially conceived just as a medical showroom, the "Medical Mart," and was the brainchild of Cleveland Clinic CEO and president Toby Cosgrove. The GCHI evolved to be the nexus of innovation, commerce, and education in healthcare.

Built with funds raised chiefly through a 0.25 percent sales tax in Cuyahoga County, the 230,000-square-foot GCHI became a physical manifestation of the region's innovation legacy and future promise. It attracted giants of the healthcare commercial world, including GE Healthcare Systems, Philips Healthcare, and Siemens, alongside unique service and technology providers to healthcare, such as Johnson Controls and Forbo Flooring Systems. When the nonprofit HIT intra-operability organization Healthcare Information and Management Systems Society (HiMSS) signed on to take an entire floor, we knew we were in business.

Other organizations represented in the GCHI are healthcare delivery institutions, most notably Cleveland Clinic, University Hospitals Health System, and MetroHealth System, our county-operated, nationally recognized trauma and acute care hospital. Traditional competitors for patients became partners to advance innovation. There are providers next to vendors, all of us looking for ways to express and optimize our innovation identities. We moved our 2,000-attendee Medical Innovation Summit to the facility in October 2013. I chair the GCHI Executive Advisory Council, and we're constantly seeking ways to leverage this singular asset to further the work we all do to bring creative thought to market to improve and extend human life.

Beyond the Cluster

As Cleveland Clinic closes in on its centennial, now a burgeoning international organization having opened a four-million-square-foot hospital in Abu Dhabi in April 2015, we are still "Cleveland's Clinic."

Clusters are the logical environments for breeding and sustaining innovation. They take respective needs and contributions and turn them into collective successes. They are catalytic and multiplicative. They are also fragile—their survival is not ensured, even when it seems like sustainability is a given.

One of the key ingredients that keep the cluster vital is the academic nucleus. Whether an AMC or research university (or both), the contributions to human and intellectual capital fuel the engine of cluster-based innovation. We need to build the concentric circles around these assets, adding commercialization capability, industry partnerships, and investor interest.

Also vital to the equation is public-sector participation. There's often a lamentable disconnect between policymaking and the generation of functioning clusters. This divide may be more a function of coordination and communication, rather than lack of cohesion. In fact, the cluster concept could, and should, be catalytic in synchronizing the stakeholders vertically and horizontally.

Policy makers from the local to federal level should grasp the concept and adopt strategies that foster innovation, while providing favorable conditions to attract business. Responsibility for cluster creation does not rely on the public sector alone. Rather, cluster creation is a dynamic interplay between the private and academic sectors set in a dynamic environment. Public involvement lowers barriers for the tenuous, evolving innovation cluster.

"What's next?" is perhaps the most frequent question asked by an innovator or entrepreneur, as well as business leaders and elected officials. Is the cluster the ultimate physical expression of innovation capability and potential? There is at least one more concentric circle that may surround and unify clusters. I can think of no more fitting term for a community of innovation stars than a constellation. What CCI has done to link institutions in the GHIA can be supersized.

We're continuously seeking creative resources and culturally aligned organizations that can work together to solve big problems for large populations. We're continuing to pioneer platforms for partnership that erase previous boundaries of competition and replace them with collaborative interaction.

A constellation could be a powerful cluster of clusters, where those dedicated to healthcare innovation can tackle the problems of access, quality, and cost together. Better yet, healthcare clusters could seek interaction with the engineering, computer science, advanced manufacturing, clean water, and energy clusters, to name a few, and cross-pollinate on an industrial scale.

Innovation is a tangible discipline. As such, it requires a home address. That home can be as narrow as the space between the ears of a creative thinker or as expansive as a global network of virtually linked innovation clusters. I'm an advocate for putting up four walls to house and protect innovation. Building a physical manifestation that demonstrates innovation's importance to those who work inside and those who pass by is an inflection point in the genesis of any successful innovation function.

When you finally get those walls erected, just be sure you spend the rest of your days breaking down any barriers they may create and continually looking outside them for good ideas and good partners.

Philanthropy

Donate Like Your Life Depends on It

The idea of giving back is appropriately named; traditional donors often are motivated retrospectively by loyalty or by a desire to repay a gratefully received benefit. There are multiple other philanthropic motivations, like supporting an organization's perpetuation for future service or enjoyment. Such motivations can be reactive, in recognition of an experience, but can also be proactive for the purpose of ensuring the institution endures to benefit the individual or wider community.

In many ways, healthcare or academic philanthropy can take either of these faces. Benefactors may give to a hospital to recognize a lifesaving service or to enable the purchase of the newest piece of medical equipment. Charity to your alma mater can be nostalgic or futuristic, or it may provide your child with an advantage in the ultracompetitive admissions process.

The common theme of these traditional philanthropy practices is that they're relatively passive. That's not to diminish the act or its importance. In many ways, this may be the purest form of generosity. There is certainly interest, but not necessarily a great deal of expectation or involvement, at least not the kind accompanied by tracking metrics and outcomes.

Philanthropists and investors have heretofore demonstrated different philosophies with regard to expected performance after they write their respective checks. Fascinatingly, we are seeing a convergence of their thinking and actions.

There's an evolving new class of philanthropists defined by two core characteristics: they *only* look forward, *and* they keep score. They go by several names, all roughly equivalent: venture philanthropist, philanthrocapitalist, and a term we coined, "pronator," as in proactive donor.

By nature, the object of the generosity of this new class of philanthropists is just the type of creative conduct taking place on the campuses of academic medical centers (AMCs) and research universities. Venture philanthropists seek high-impact investments, especially where they can measure outcome.

There are three types of venture philanthropist who are not only generous with their gifts but also seek to participate in the commercialization of technologies supported by their generosity:

- The eponymous foundation funder

- The mission-driven subscriber

- The inventor-philanthropist

The Eponymous Foundation Funder

The poster child for venture philanthropy is the high-net-worth family or individual. Names such as Bill Gates, Sir

Richard Branson, and Charles "Chuck" Feeney are known internationally, but each city has generous citizens who have endowed assets in the arts, education, and healthcare. Many have established eponymous foundations as the vehicle for giving to solve big problems for large populations.

What defines these individuals as venture philanthropists is their level of involvement in the work of their beneficiaries.[1] Venture philanthropists don't just write the check; their engagement means they also leverage their expertise and resources to produce a desired societal outcome. Lending their names to an issue or opportunity gives it weight and provides a gravitational pull.

The pool of venture philanthropists is growing. The number of billionaires has more than doubled to 1,646 since the financial crisis of 2008.[2]

The new wealth created by technology-based innovation, combined with this attitude of engaged giving, has created interest in sponsoring mission-driven innovation. For example, the Bill & Melinda Gates Foundation supports projects with potential for big breakthroughs in improving global health and industrial development, enhancing American education, and furthering basic research.[3] The theme is unmistakable: innovation is a worthwhile target for giving.

Many philanthropists make gifts to unquestionably worthy causes, such as breast cancer or child welfare; these essentially are the fruits of innovation's toils. The mission-driven innovation infrastructure is like a fertile farm, and many philanthropists are starting to recognize that. What's emerging via venture philanthropy is that a donor can direct a gift to the innovation engine itself, essentially investing in the basic soil and water that produces breakthrough advancement in multiple disciplines. Such support for innovation infrastructure can ensure a sustainable pipeline of solutions across many disciplines and diseases.

The impact of this evolving concept could be enormous. There are nearly 75,000 private U.S. foundations, accounting for nearly a trillion dollars in assets and grants of about $50 billion annually. Private foundation funding now ranks below only government grants in supporting scholarly pursuits in AMCs and research universities.[4]

Some eponymous foundation funders go beyond incentivizing outcomes to sharing in profits generated by the work they fund. The returns do not accrue until the net profits from the development exceed the level of the contribution, but there is a tax benefit at the time of donation. This may be a uniquely attractive avenue for venture philanthropists who seek to "do well and do good."

The Mission-Driven Subscriber

Not all philanthropists supporting innovation are multi-millionaires. Perhaps the most promising group consists of your coworkers, neighbors, and friends who support a cause by donating small amounts through vehicles ranging from credit card transactions and PayPal to sophisticated, dedicated crowdfunding sites.

Internet platforms are emerging that link the beneficiary and benefactor. Indiegogo, Kickstarter, RocketHub, and Razoo, to name a few, have developed significant traction in the crowdfunding space. Originally serving the artistic community, the power of these vehicles is beginning to be understood in research and innovation circles. The Internet also has fostered self-directed information gathering and no-pressure decision making regarding investing in a cause, organization, or innovation.

A cluster of thousands can donate an aggregated million dollars to assist an independent movie director in making a film. Can the same tactic be modified so that an innovator can further research toward a commercial outcome and potentially cure millions? How do we identify, educate, and activate the engaged masses already inclined to support innovation? Their bank accounts may not be as robust as the glitterati described earlier, but the zeal for solutions to pressing problems qualifies these investors as cognoscenti.

This new micro-giving community simultaneously seeks connection and convenience. These donors want to feel like they're uniquely in the know, while being part of something. They're enabled by the anonymity of technology to satisfy all of these communal, educational, and transactional aspects.

Cleveland Clinic has been investigating how this new economy can be adapted to further innovation. The existing model of crowdfunding is characterized by the interaction of project initiators, funders, and platform operators. Their roles are fairly straightforward, and the basic economics varies little. Essentially, an equity exchange takes place between the initiator and the funder(s), while the platform operators collect a transactional fee.

There is increasing interest in tapping this milieu to gain a fresh source of financial support for embryonic ideas and emerging companies. Concerns about intellectual property (IP) protection, effect on patentability, or risk to proprietary competitive advantage are real but manageable.

While studying this model for adaptability to Cleveland Clinic, we recognized a characteristic that might open up new possibilities. The typical crowdfunding model has an intermediary, the platform operator, which is truly not connected to the projects it represents. Cleveland Clinic suggested that the medium could be the mission[5]—to link the crowd directly with innovators.

We're preparing to launch our PRONATE™ platform, which will allow potential givers to peruse a portfolio of projects, follow and support individual innovators, or choose to fund the operational infrastructure that serves all of our inventors. We have disintermediated the platform operators, who were already detached. Only an innovation engine could bring this level of intimacy to the transaction.

PRONATE™ also will combine the worlds of crowdfunding and crowdsourcing. The terms *crowdsourcing* and *open innovation*, often used interchangeably, are used here to describe the solicitation of intellectual contributions toward the solution of identified challenges.

The Inventor-Philanthropist

Building a robust commercialization engine is not without its challenges and resource demands. I have yet to find an innovator on the Cleveland Clinic staff or a partner in our global alliance who takes for granted the complex infrastructure and dedicated professionals composing Cleveland Clinic Innovations (CCI). The machinery of innovation described throughout this book is an asset to which all partners have direct access. We're in constant communication with our clients, the inventors, both about the gestation of their individual technologies and how we can improve our development services.

In less resource-rich environments, it must be challenging and frustrating for prolific creators, especially those with "day jobs," to advance their innovations to the marketplace. For this subset of inventors, we've developed a protocol and mechanism by which they may access the services of CCI and our alliance partners. Because our flywheels are spinning, it's relatively easy to accommodate spikes in volume.

Our first step in such relationships is to ascertain what IP policies govern the inventors' contributions. If no policy is in place, or a favorable arrangement can be made that permits the inventor access to CCI's capabilities, we discuss what form a disclosure may take. In general, the approach can be characterized as commercial or charitable. The former is straightforward and resembles the typical inventor and distribution policies followed by our organization. We have two models for charitably directed IP disclosures: traditional donation and revenue sharing.

- **Traditional donation.** The inventor-philanthropist donates his or her IP to the institution. The benefactor may receive tax considerations for the basis in which he or she invested in development of the IP up to the date of its donation. We always insist that donors consult their tax professionals before embarking on this path.

- **Revenue sharing.** The mechanism to establish value for the donor's tax purposes is identical to the traditional donation and is based on the inventor-donor's basis in the donated technology—not its market value at the time of the donation. The difference arises in revenue distribution from subsequent commercial activity, and will depend on the individual circumstances and the prevailing tax law. After the inventor's basis is eclipsed by the net proceeds from transactions, (i.e., a royalty-bearing license or sale of the company), we are exploring the potential of dividing the proceeds according to a prescribed formula, usually derived from existing inventor distribution policies.

The reason to explore this new field at the nexus of philanthropy and innovation is that many inventors don't have ready access to the mid- to late-development apparatus that institutions like Cleveland Clinic have established. The innovator with a charitable penchant may realize short-term benefits from favorable tax consideration. The innovation function and host institution receives something of value that they are uniquely capable of enhancing through our professional processes.

The revenue-sharing option, if approved by the IRS and exercised by the donor, satisfies both the philanthropic and entrepreneurial spirits. It's the cousin of the venture philanthropist profit-sharing option described earlier, but the inventor-philanthropists donate IP rather than funds. They remain involved strategically and financially, while creating tangible advantage for Cleveland Clinic. It's also attractive to alumni motivated by loyalty to an academic institution, as well as furthering innovation.

The inaugural example of the inventor-philanthropist model was the donation that my wife, CeCe, and I made in 2011. We donated a suite of IP developed while I was away from Cleveland Clinic for a decade. Preparing to return as the organization's first chief innovation officer, I sought to organize my inventor/entrepreneur portfolio and was particularly sensitive to potential conflict-of-interest issues. I had a cohesive collection of more than 30 patented medical devices that would benefit from CCI's development process. I had documented costs of legal, engineering, prototyping, and regulatory opinions. I also had independent market valuations of the IP performed, which well exceeded my basis of investment. To reiterate, the present tax laws will focus on the inventor's investment in the development of the technology prior to its donation, *not* the perceived market valuation. It is imperative that each individual contemplating a donation of this type consult with his or her tax professionals.

CCI established the model by which I, as inventor, would donate the IP to Cleveland Clinic and be credited with the amount of my previous investment for tax purposes. In addition to an increased number of patents, the benefit to Cleveland

Clinic was that I had previously absorbed much of the initial development cost. My initial benefit was that the IP received professional development assistance from acknowledged leaders in the innovation field, as well as favorable tax consideration for the donation related to the amount I had invested.

Already, this has stimulated others to donate over $2.5 million of valuable IP. The concept is working for everybody, especially the patients who will be served ultimately by a new infusion of IP having greater likelihood of reaching the market and their bedside.

Conclusion

We often hear that an individual has a "gift for innovation," reflecting an innate capacity or talent for relevant creativity. In this chapter, I described the "gift for innovation" in a different context. Linking the innovator and the generous benefactor is making an important margin of difference at Cleveland Clinic.

A recent example from Cleveland Clinic represents such an engaged, passionate giver. The work of immunologist Vincent K. Tuohy in developing a breast cancer vaccine so inspired Iris and the late Mort November that they endowed a research chair for $1 million. They learned about his groundbreaking research, contacted Dr. Tuohy, and funded the chair, adding to their considerable generosity to Cleveland Clinic that has included the Debra Ann November Pediatric Airway and Pulmonary Mechanics Lab and the Debra Ann November Wing at the Center for Autism at Cleveland Clinic. Highly engaged in Dr. Tuohy's work, the Novembers made an investment in his game-changing endeavor to increase its chances of improving and saving human lives.

Philanthropy directed toward innovation is a novel way to express generosity. It's also a logical funding target for individuals enriched by technology-sector success, the motivated and informed advocate for certain issues, and the inventor inclined toward philanthropy.

In addition to generosity, the other trait that links these philanthropists is their level of engagement. These are active givers who want to see discipline exercised around the handling of their funds but still understand that the vicissitudes of innovation don't always produce success.

CCI has been a pioneer in uniting innovators and philanthropists. We shall continue to find ways to give forward—the unique capability of innovation and the philanthropists who support it—to donate like your life depends on it.

Predictions

The Future of Healthcare Innovation

What's coming down the pike? Everyone's fascinated by the next new thing and developing trends. The reasons are obvious, and in healthcare, the stakes are always high. Impacts felt on Wall Street and Main Street include dollars, jobs, and lives saved.

The innovator must be a patient futurist, balancing enthusiasm and realism. A key requirement is accepting failure, while working toward a goal that's often elusive. We're building the future of medicine in a systematic, logical fashion.

The crystal ball and magic wand can illustrate the difference between what outsiders believe we do and how those in innovation see their jobs. The crystal ball is a simple lens into the future; the magic wand is a tool for channeling special talent and expertise. While having a real-time glimpse into impending genius is a privilege, innovation isn't a passive exercise. We're actively influencing the attributes and availability of next-generation technologies.

Sometimes I think the process is magic, because my colleagues seem to pull off great feats with intellectual and technical aplomb. In truth, it's expertise, multiplied by elbow grease. What would be truly magical is to involve more stakeholders, especially the industry and investment community, at the early stages of innovation in our academic medical centers (AMCs) and research universities.

The Argument for Value-Based Innovation

In Chapter 5, I described the "Value of Medical Innovation." The perspective there was to defend the notion that innovation, on the whole, made the delivery of medical care a more expensive proposition by adding costs for the development and deployment of new diagnostic and therapeutic modalities.

In this section, a small manipulation of the words to "Value-Based Innovation" seeks to represent the new movement in creative development that now takes into account the ultimate fiscal impact and appeal of innovations from the outset of the commercialization process.

Early on when innovating orthopaedic medical devices, colleagues and I joked that we'd advance a plate or prosthetic implant by "making it out of solid gold." Flashier, complex, and more expensive seemed innovative. It's easy to fall in love with your own ideas, especially if they reflect some level of sophistication that sets it (or presumably, the inventor) apart. That type of thinking is being squeezed out of innovation, and rightly so. The new paradigm is to deliver products and processes that increase access, improve outcomes, *and* demonstrate fiscal responsibility in healthcare delivery.

Cleveland Clinic is in the vanguard of Value-Based Care, moving from volume-driven, episodic, and expensive care delivery to managing populations efficiently and effectively. Simply, *value* can be defined by change in clinical outcome divided by cost of care. If medicine is moving to a value basis, so should innovation. As a pioneer in mission-driven innovation, Cleveland Clinic Innovations (CCI) is logically positioned to write the next chapter in commercialization and corporate venturing, value-based innovation.

The cost of innovation can be calculated, but its net effect is practically incalculable. I've spent my career trying to correct the misperception that innovation is expensive—or adds expense to the medical system. You can probably track expense, but it's impossible to compute impact. The cost of developing penicillin could be tallied, but how could you determine the payback in restoration to health and lives saved?

We developed a working description for value-based innovation: *Delivering solutions for big problems affecting large populations more quickly, more efficiently, and less expensively.* This is the inverse of beliefs at the beginning of my career, when expense to the system was not particularly considered. Now, fiscal responsibility shares priority with potential for positively affecting patients.

The Future of Financing Healthcare Innovation

It's difficult to bring a promising idea from the bedside to the bank. The novel concept must demonstrate clinical and scientific merit and receive significant capital infusions at critical times. It is almost unheard of for a single source of capital to finance emerging concepts from beginning to end. Instead, the investments are syndicated—multiple funding sources must be matched to development stage, size of investment, and risk tolerance.

For mission-driven innovations, initial capital typically comes from the institutions in which the ideas originate. It can be a scramble for the innovation team to assemble sufficient initial resources from various internal sources, such as research accounts, funds earmarked for innovation, philanthropic sources, and dollars directed at the CEO's discretion. Even in institutions lacking a well-developed innovation function, I remain impressed that backing for the best ideas usually is secured.

However, relying on institutional resources is too unpredictable and inefficient. Innovation executives must seek stable assets such as grants. The federal government has traditionally been a player, through recognized funding mechanisms such as the National Institutes of Health (NIH). Individual states are starting to play an expanded role in catalyzing innovation through grants and loans that stimulate regional economic development. Federal and state leaders recognize innovation as a worthy pursuit, along with discovery science, because it creates jobs and stimulates the tax base.

Participation of Federal and State Government in Innovation

Cleveland Clinic has benefitted from federal and state government funds. The following examples represent some of the ways government funding stimulates commercialization of our promising ideas.

- **Ohio Third Frontier (OTF).** Established in 2002 and extended through at least 2015, this $2.1 billion strategic initiative focuses on creating and sustaining a statewide innovation ecosystem. Funds support the efficient transition of great ideas from the laboratory to the marketplace. The OTF uses an established award process to identify high-performing organizations and promising technologies that will benefit from critical capital infusions. An engaged, experienced 11-member commission and 16-member advisory board guide the investments. More than 60 percent of OTF dollars are directed toward healthcare and bioscience innovation and company attraction. This includes Entrepreneurial Signature Programs (ESPs) that support biomedical technology-based commercialization.

CCI has been the grateful recipient of nearly $175 million, the highest percentage of funds directed to the healthcare and bioscience community. This has allowed us to establish the Global Cardiovascular Innovation Center (GCIC), our collaborative of six Ohio-based AMCs and research universities,[1] among other worthwhile projects. The GCIC has become an international leader in developing, acquiring, incubating, and commercializing technologies that improve the care of diseases and disorders of the heart and blood vessels. The GCIC is located in the offices of CCI, along with about 25 of our incubating companies.

- **JobsOhio.** This is a private, nonprofit corporation designed to lead Ohio's job-creation efforts by singularly focusing on attracting and retaining jobs, with an emphasis on strategic industry sectors in areas of statewide and regional strength. Using a private-sector approach, JobsOhio works at the speed of business, enabling Ohio to be more nimble and flexible and thus more competitive in its economic development efforts

- **NIH Centers for Accelerated Innovations (NCAI).** These centers offer a one-stop shop to accelerate translation of early-stage technologies for further development by the private sector and ultimately commercialization. The National Heart, Lung, and Blood Institute dedicated $31.5 million to establish three inaugural multi-institutional centers, including the NIH Center for Accelerated Innovations at Cleveland Clinic. The NIH believes that patient care and public health can be advanced by fostering collaboration to translate basic science advancements into commercially viable products.

Innovation executives must be adept at identifying and accessing governmental resources such as these. Securing capital from sources that seek returns in jobs, rather than simply in revenue, can be transformative. We foresee more federal programs being directed toward innovation and that additional states will follow the lead of Ohio.

As I project the future of innovation funding, absent thus far is how to activate the industrial sector and investment community. Careful consideration and nimble execution are required to reintroduce these funders to true early-stage innovation, as venture (and even angel) investors have largely abandoned the mission-driven, organic innovation milieu.

Can Venture Capital Be Reengaged in Mission-Driven Innovation?

Mission-driven innovators and the investment community have a symbiotic relationship that historically has defined the innovation ecosystem. We use similar financial measures to track our performance, and both seek to produce results and work together. Even the most ardent innovators take a respite from describing their technology to count how much money it has raised or the number of blue-chip investors pursuing it!

But over the past decade, adverse market forces exposed tension between those who build the engine and those who supply financial fuel to make it run. The entire issue is sum-marized in the frequent investor lament, heard when we seek capital for nascent technologies, "Your material is *too early* and *too risky*."

It can be difficult to counter the argument that medical innovation is expensive, risky, and long-to-market. Investors often see only the meter running on the costs of innovation and can't calculate the human or economic impact of new ideas. These barriers don't deter the mission-driven innovator from pursuing solutions to help humankind, but the investor still looks for returns.

Traditional venture capital has practically disengaged from the earliest and most vulnerable evolution process of new technologies. That's a bold statement and truly not meant to diminish, deter, or disparage the venture community. It's simply a fact that innovation leaders must accept and for which they must plan accordingly.

The venture-capital business demonstrated considerable contraction after the dot-com boom of the early 2000s, as illustrated in Figure 10.1. While the media reports signs of a rebound, the mission-driven innovation community remains concerned.

Invariably, when you drill down to what venture investors believe is investable, it's usually companies just starting to record robust, sustainable revenues. The focus of even "smart capital" has become those few companies emerging from "the valley of death" to continue the journey toward the market-place. Today, the early-stage definition is truly all over the map, from $2 million in revenue to north of $20 million.

I'm cautiously optimistic about the venture commu-nity. The recent surge in activity is tied largely to the more capital-efficient health information technology (HIT) startups. Big data and virtual goods and services have the promise of attracting investment closer to the starting line of

FIGURE 10.1 Trends in Venture Capital Under Management

	1993	2003	2013
No. of Professionals	5,217	14,777	5,891
No. of First Time VC Funds Raised	25	34	53
No. of VC Funds Raising Money This Year	93	160	187
VC Capital Raised This Year ($B)	4.5	9.1	16.8
VC Capital Under Management ($B)	29.3	263.9	192.9
Avg VC Capital Under Mgt per Firm ($M)	79.2	277.5	220.7
Avg VC Fund Size to Date ($M)	40.2	94.4	110.3
Avg VC Fund Size Raised This Year ($M)	48.3	102.9	89.7
Largest VC Fund Raised to Date ($M)	1,775.0	6,300.0	6,300.0

Source: National Venture Capital Association Yearbook

development. Even therapeutics and diagnostics is demonstrating some unique models that marry the investment and commercial players.

Attracting Industry Back to Innovation with Sophisticated Financial Modeling

There's a squeeze on funding within academic medicine resulting from the U.S. Patient Protection and Affordable Care Act (PPACA), and dwindling grant-making capabilities from historical government funders affect our colleagues in higher education. This leaves mission-driven innovation with a vital challenge: to innovate the financing model for innovation.

A mechanism must be developed to sustain the basic architecture of innovation at the AMC and research university. The first requirement is to agree on the definition of what the mission-driven innovation community actually does, how we do it, and what we aspire to accomplish.

Then we can work on reengaging our most intimate partner in innovation—the industries with whom we interface on
a daily basis in a number of different venues. The way to do
so is through a mechanism with two key components: ideas
and capital. Exchanging ideas as currency is more straightforward to understand; we have a history of codeveloping
technologies with industry partners and also welcome their
intellectual properties (IP) into our innovation portfolio for
further development.

But this is about attracting capital for the earliest stages
of technology development. In the process of managing
large amounts of IP from Cleveland Clinic and our Global
Healthcare Innovations Alliance (GHIA) partners, it
became increasingly clear that raising funds for each idea
was exceedingly difficult and inefficient. This led to our concept of managing via a portfolio approach, each containing
hundreds of gestating ideas, and spreading resources over
our four CCI domains of medical devices, therapeutics and
diagnostics, HIT, and delivery solutions. The portfolios have
intersections such as orthopaedic medical device or cancer
drugs. Some boxes are more populous than others, but there
are developing opportunities in almost every intersection.

Through a stroke of serendipity, the idea of a "mutual
fund" of innovation assets was coalescing about the time I
was introduced to MIT Sloan School of Management finance
professor Andrew Lo.

Dr. Lo is a rock-star economist, deservedly named to
Time magazine's 2012 list of The World's 100 Most Influential
People for his multidisciplinary approach to finance, using
everything from statistical analysis to neuroscience to better
understand markets. His theory on "adaptive markets," in
which he likens investing in innovation to messy biological
systems, is genius and shows an extraordinary understanding
of the entire ecosystem.

In a landmark 2012 paper in *Nature Biotechnology*,[2] Dr. Lo and colleagues identified that large pharmaceutical concerns were distancing themselves from participation in early-stage drug development. They observed that minus 1 percent returns over the past decade had caused venture capitalists to disengage from most healthcare and bioscience startups. The resulting capital gap was diminishing U.S. innovation potential, threatening our nation's ability to produce potentially lifesaving solutions to today's and tomorrow's diseases.

Dr. Lo proposed a megafund funneling up to $30 billion toward the development of new drugs, particularly those for cancer treatment. He correctly observed that the entire innovation ecosystem was ripe for something new and that securitization with a fund of unprecedented scale could unite the IP development engines of AMCs and research universities, while connecting the large pharmaceutical companies and drawing new investors to the early stages of drug creation.

In exchange for a small percentage of licensing revenue resulting from the new level of organic innovation, a win-win-win strategy would result. Academic engines would get the resources needed to continue to innovate at the most organic stages. Pharmaceutical companies would replenish their pipelines of new drugs. Dormant investors would see the spigot start to flow again, with returns tied not to a single blockbuster, but to more predictable, sustainable royalty revenues from a collection of new drugs. As mission-driven innovators, we recognized another group that would win—patients.

I was introduced to Dr. Lo by Dennis M. Kass, a member of our Innovation Advisory Board who's become a close friend. Dennis had a distinguished public service career in the Reagan administration and a subsequent equally illustrious career in private-sector finance. Dr. Lo and Dennis not only are brilliant financial minds, their personal philosophies of integrity, benevolence, and generosity qualify them as mission-driven innovators.

Our thoughts began to clarify regarding how to bring all stakeholders in the innovation ecosystem together to ensure adequate, sustainable funding, not only for cancer drugs, but for the entire portfolio of gestating IP in our matrix.

Admittedly, the soufflé hasn't yet risen, but the interest and enthusiasm for bringing sophisticated financial engineering concepts to the innovation ecosystem is considerable. We're currently exploring how securitization and other financial engineering theories could revolutionize the funding of innovation in AMCs and research universities. Presently, Cleveland Clinic and MIT are engaged in building models to solve what could be the biggest threat to American creativity, the lack of adequate capital to develop it. It's not only an opportunity for two great institutions to work together to change the face of innovation, but a responsibility to leverage our strengths on behalf of the entire community. Even venture philanthropists have expressed interest in this potential sponsorship of the innovation infrastructure that could lead to healthcare improvement across all domains.

CCI's engagement with Dr. Lo emphasizes that innovation isn't confined to drug discovery or medical device development. We must seek intersections of knowledge domains where innovation is most fertile, looking across all economic sectors.

This demonstrates the uniting force of mission. When the purpose is to improve and extend human life, the reason to connect is compelling and cannot simply be reduced to dollars invested or earned. However, we need to be aware of the costs and potential economic impacts, which makes innovating the way dollars flow around our ecosystem a priority for all stakeholders.

Picking the Winners: Summit and Top 10

At Cleveland Clinic, we engage in predictions at our annual Medical Innovation Summit, forecasting future healthcare advances. It provides an unrivaled perspective on evolving medical solutions and financial drivers in healthcare and bioscience. While there is an annual theme, for example, neuroscience in 2015, the summit serves as the recognized platform for interaction on all topics relevant to the world of mission-driven innovation and healthcare transformation.

The buzz that puts each annual summit at the front of business sections and news broadcasts around the country is our annual Top 10 Innovations. We share the evolving technologies that CCI leaders have identified as the most promising candidates to shape healthcare delivery over the next 12 months. Our team interviews more than 100 Cleveland Clinic and global alliance caregivers to elicit their nominations. We then employ a rigorous process to distill the opinions of Cleveland Clinic physicians and researchers, identify a roster of nominated technologies, and develop a consensus perspective of what will be the leading medical innovations for the coming year.

Nominated technologies must offer significant patient benefit in comparison to current practices, have a high probability of commercial success, and be on the market in the coming year. Adhering to our disciplined approach to every facet of medical innovation, we follow our selected technologies and keep score on how our process performed in picking the winners. It's fascinating to see how accurate our experts prove to be.[3]

Ingenuity Will Create Prosperity

The political climate around the PPACA is divisive enough without considering its potential adverse effects on the medical innovation ecosystem. Some of the legislation is quite damaging, such as the 2.3 percent excise tax on medical devices manufactured in the United States or imported (Section 4191 of the Internal Revenue Code). However, there is reason to believe that ingenuity will always create prosperity, despite headwinds.

Data and popular sentiment both indicate that the pressures of Obamacare to deliver and pay for services in nontraditional ways have created pockets of opportunity in digital health, primary care, consumer-driven healthcare, and even around the concepts of risk sharing. The brightest minds have been at work for several years to determine how to identify the true barriers the legislation has erected and create fixes that improve access, quality, outcome, and cost.

To be an innovator is to be a futurist. We don't simply peer into the unknown of tomorrow, we work to shape it. The realities of the new healthcare economy may create challenges, but if we stick to our mission and reach out for collaborators, we will advance healthcare. There is not a single solution, nor an isolated group, that could shoulder the expectation of optimizing medical innovation in the new millennium. Instead, we need input from all stakeholders and recognition from key supporters to continue to produce game-changing technologies.

We're All Going to Be Patients

In 2012, at age 50, a gallstone lodged in my pancreas and exploded it, an extremely rare and ordinarily fatal medical problem. I spent six months hovering between life and death in Cleveland Clinic's operating rooms and intensive care units. For the first three months of my hospitalization, the real possibility was that each day might be my last. When I turned the first corner and thought I might survive, it was a time of jubilation. But it was doubtful I would resume a normal life, and my family and I were planning for long-term care options. A couple months further into the journey, my continued improvement surprised everyone, who now believed I would eventually leave the hospital, but likely not work again. Well, in the last month of my campaign, my care-givers did such a wonderful job that I was targeting a time when I would resume my duties as Cleveland Clinic's chief innovation officer.

What I learned over the course of this ordeal has afforded me a unique perspective on the medical system and on the importance of innovation.

- **Make relentless forward progress.** As a patient, it seemed sometimes that survival was a matter of choice, but I never gave up. The same goes for the innovator. If a project doesn't work out, get back on the horse with fervor and enthusiasm. Whether it's your life that's on the line, or your ideas that could affect the lives of others, you can't be defeatist.

- **You must have an advocate.** It's difficult for a patient to go it alone; you need a team of doctors, nurses, other caregivers, and loved ones. Neither can you go it alone as an inventor. You need the support of colleagues, collaborators, and your organization's innovation leaders. Find your individual innovation champion, someone who takes an interest in you and your ideas.

- **You should be overseen by a team.** Expert care-givers working together across the lines of medical specialty translates into better patient outcomes. Similarly, a strong innovation function displays quality of leadership and level of collaboration. Seek an organization where the staff and innovation function work as a team to develop and bring ideas to market.

- **You will need every possible source of strength.** As a patient, you need the support of everyone with whom you come in contact. The power of a small gesture can be immense: a touch of the hand, sitting by your hospital bed so you can communicate at eye level. Just as I needed the gravitational pull of many to come back from the brink, innovation needs a boost from every possible sector it touches, from elected officials and philanthropists to the business and investment communities. Even patients must become more ardent advocates.

- **Life is an algorithm.** As a patient, your recovery will be the sum of a thousand choices. Strive to be compliant, not complicated. Trust your caregivers and their expert consensus. Innovation is a journey with a thousand forks in the road and almost as many potholes. Prepare for more than a few side trips. Let the journey be its own reward, and put trust in the professionals handling your case. Accepting ambiguity and delay will free you to think nimbly when course correction is required.

I learned before discharge that because of my 20 surgeries, I would never play golf again. I protested, "Why didn't you tell me this was serious?" To be clear, there is nothing that can supplant the desire to return to your family after you've faced death, but vocational challenges and avocational pleasures are additional vital motivators.

During the months I was staring at the ceiling tiles, I tried to recall golf courses I had played to both exercise my mind and inspire myself to one day resume play. A return to Pine Valley Golf Club in New Jersey, my favorite cathedral of the game and one of its toughest physical challenges, would indicate that I had regained a normal life. I was lucky to make it back to Pine Valley the summer following my discharge.

I was granted life's ultimate mulligan, so now I must live up to deserving it. I may have contributed modestly to the field of innovation, but I'm one of the most grateful recipients of its munificence. Innovation saved my life.

What I have learned in a lifetime that has cast me as a physician, innovator, and patient is that we play the ball where it lies. It's challenging to script the longitudinal progression through any of these pursuits, but the chance of success is maximized by discipline, process, and collaboration. There are few guarantees in any engagement, certainly not in innovation, but one practical surety is that we will all be patients. It will be innovation that helps you or your loved ones live longer and better.

Innovation matters to each of us. Some look through the lens of the inventor, doggedly pursuing incremental or disruptive improvement in the status quo. The investor may see opportunity and return on innovation. Those of us responsible for the innovation ecosystem, at our organizations and across the world, seek to balance the requirements of stakeholders while adhering to institutional mission.

Regardless of your position in the mission-driven innovation universe, we all convene at the same point, the patient. Whether you're a patient or an innovator, your ultimate success cannot be delivered without collaboration. It's the responsibility of leaders in the mission-driven innovation ecosystem to be the catalyst to bring all the complex components together.

CCI is proud to be a pioneer and leading practitioner of mission-driven innovation. We're honored to represent our institutional identity and serve our inventors. We will tirelessly continue to bring about healthcare transformation and service to our partners. I want you to join me, the Cleveland Clinic, and our Global Healthcare Innovation Alliance partners in pursuit of solutions to transform healthcare and improve lives. The ideas deserve it, the innovators deserve it, and the patients deserve it.

Invention Disclosure Form

Cleveland Clinic
Innovations

Lead the Way

innovations

Invention Disclosure Form

Cleveland Clinic Invention Disclosure Form

INVENTOR DETAILS: If there are more than 3 inventors, please use a separate sheet.

List all persons who have directly contributed in the development or conception of the invention. **All individuals who have made any inventive contribution must be listed for a valid patent application to be filed. For Delivery Solutions inventions, list Institute/Department contacts.**

	INVENTOR 1 (*Lead Inventor)	INVENTOR 2	INVENTOR 3
FULL NAME			
CC DEPARTMENT & INSTITUTE			
HOME ADDRESS (Please provide Street Address, City, State and Zip)			
PHONE			
EMAIL			
COUNTRY OF CITIZENSHIP			
EMPLOYEE #			
DATE OF BIRTH			
% CONTRIBUTION**			
SIGNATURE			

DEPARTMENT CHAIR	DEPARTMENT/DIVISION	DATE	SIGNATURE

*The Lead Inventor will be Innovations' main contact for the invention and is responsible for sharing correspondence with other inventors listed on this document and assisting in the completion of tasks.

** % Contribution indicates the percentage that each inventor should receive from the inventor share of the commercialization revenue. % Contribution should not be completed for Delivery Solutions inventions that are developed as part of an Institutional or Departmental initiative.
Assignment: By signing this invention disclosure, each Cleveland Clinic inventor hereby assigns all rights, titles and interests to The Cleveland Clinic Foundation and denotes that the inventor also agrees to cooperate in the filing of patent applications and the commercialization of the technology.

Send the completed, signed form and all attachments to:
disclosure@ccf.org or Cleveland Clinic Innovations GCIC-10

Cleveland Clinic   Invention Disclosure Form

Title of Invention	
Date of Invention (conception)	

TAXONOMY

From what area(s) below would a Peer Review Committee provide the most relevant clinical and technical feedback on your invention?

Clinical Application

☐ Anesthesia	Imaging	Pediatrics
Cancer	Medicine	Respiratory
Dermatology & Plastics	Neurological	Urology
Digestive Disease	Nursing	Wellness
Emergency Services	OBGYN/Women's Health	Other
Endocrinology	Ophthalmology	
Head and Neck	Orthopedics	
Heart & Vascular	Pathology/Lab Medicine	

Invention Domain (select one)

Medical Device	Health Information Technology (HIT)*
Therapeutics & Diagnostics	Delivery Solutions**

*HIT: computer hardware/software dealing with the storage, retrieval, sharing, and use of health care information, data, and knowledge

**Delivery Solution: clinical and/or business process know-how

Cleveland Clinic

INVENTION DETAILS

1. Provide a description of the invention.

2. Add images. Click to Attach

INVENTION DETAILS (continued)

3. What problem does the invention solve and what are the advantages of the invention over other known technologies or solutions (please list)?

4. Stage of Development & Technical Feasibility: Describe the current state of development and availability of technology necessary to develop and commercialize the invention. (Have prototypes been built or proof of concept otherwise been established? Describe any bench, preclinical, or clinical testing performed to date.)

5. Has there been or is there a plan for any public disclosure of the invention? If yes, please explain.

6. Are there any experts at Cleveland Clinic or elsewhere that should provide input on this invention?

7. List any information known about existing patents, publications or other prior art relevant to the invention.

SOURCES OF FUNDING

Please identify any financial sponsors of the invention, as well as the relevant grant/contract numbers. Include Institutional or Department funding and any applicable corresponding Institutional or Department initiative.

FUNDING SOURCE (Federal Agency, Society, Organization, etc.)	GRANT, CONTRACT NUMBER, OR INSTITUTIONAL/DEPARTMENTAL INITIATIVE

CC is required to report government funded inventions to relevant funding agencies and provide a written description of the invention in technical detail (please see link for more information).

Appendix A

INVENTOR TECHNOLOGY ASSESSMENT FORM

For all inventions, please answer the following questions as completely as possible for
consideration by the Peer Review Committee.

1. How would this technology benefit patients' health outcomes?

2. What clinical criteria must patients meet before they can become candidates for use of
   this technology?

3. Indicate relevant peer-reviewed journal references that support the efficacy, safety and
   clinical need of the proposed technology.

4. What medical associations, consensus panels, and/or other technology assessment bodies
   would evaluate the safety and efficacy of this technology?

Appendix A

INVENTOR TECHNOLOGY ASSESSMENT FORM (continued)

5. **What are the specific indications and methods of use for which this technology would receive FDA market clearance or approval?**

6. **How would patient outcomes using this technology compare to the available alternatives?**

7. **Estimate this technology's estimated yearly volume of use.**

8. **How would the cost of this technology compare to the alternatives?**

Cleveland Clinic   Invention Disclosure Form

Appendix B   Supplemental Information - Optional

HEALTH INFORMATION TECHNOLOGY

The following questions apply to HIT Inventions only.

9.   Are there any open-source elements included/embedded in the Source Code? Please list.

10. Describe language used to develop applications and platforms on which the software will run. Is it easily portable to other platforms? Does it require other products/software to run? What are the system requirements for the software?

11. Are there any documents/manuals describing the software and its operation? If so, please include.

The Road to Drug Approval

T he U.S. Food and Drug Administration (FDA) drug approval process has nine stages (fda.gov). They are organic research; target identification and validation; determination of a lead compound; ADME/tox testing; compound optimization; preclinical testing; investigational new drug (IND) application; clinical trials (Phases 1, 2, and 3); new drug application (NDA); manufacture and scaling; and Phase 4 testing. Each step is described in detail in this appendix, with an eye to how it contributes to the ultimate expense of drug development (see fda.gov).

Organic Research

The initial step is a characterization of the disease or disorder that is in need of a new therapeutic approach. Academic medical centers (AMCs) such as Cleveland Clinic might seem to have an advantage in problem identification because of the volume and variety of the pathologies, but the understanding of disease processes isn't limited to AMCs. Research universities, government laboratories, and industry-based scientists all are toiling to produce meaningful discovery science.

The understanding of basic chemistry, genetics, protein synthesis, and even potential chemical interactions informs initial paths. In addition to knowledge, there is also the need for insight; it takes a level of sagacity to understand a disease process and its relationship to a new drug treatment.

Target Identification and Validation

Understanding a disease needing treatment with a new drug therapy and selection of a molecular target is like looking at something with the naked eye versus an electron microscope. The target must be as focal as a single molecule, protein, or gene.

The target must also be "drugable," meaning a new compound can influence its operation, block its synthesis, or alter its expression. Early studies that establish some form of cause and effect are crucial. If a specific molecule can be implicated in a disease and shown to be influenced or modified by a drug family, then it may be worthwhile to allocate resources to the process of drug discovery.

Determination of a Lead Compound

The processes thus far can be characterized as basic research and development. But once the search for a specific molecule commences, innovators are pursuing drug discovery. Whether it's through observation of natural phenomena, creation at the bench or computer of molecules with certain structural characteristics, or high throughput screening, filters are necessary to identify the lead compound.

Lead compound designation is not equivalent to calling a newly identified molecule, whether discovered or synthesized, a new medicine. An extraordinary volume of lengthy, expensive testing awaits.

ADME/Tox Testing

Pharmacokinetics refers to how the body handles exogenous substances. The evaluation of lead compounds consists of a battery of tests to determine how the body will respond to and tolerate the substance. The acronym ADME/tox represents what innovators and scientists consider when sifting through lead compounds: absorption, distribution, metabolism, excretion, and toxicity.

Compound Optimization

Lead compound selection is both a winnowing and a tweaking process. Sophisticated medicinal chemists can alter subtly the structure of molecules to behave differently regarding any of the ADME/tox criteria.

Fortunately, much of this work can now be performed on high-powered computers through finite element analysis rather than arduous and repetitive bench testing, but the concept is the same, and trial and error still plays an important role. Dozens or even hundreds of analogs can be tested to determine the influence a small chemical alteration has on the molecule's performance. Because this is typically the step before preclinical trials, many experienced drug developers consider some of the practical ramifications of altering the chemistry. These include, but are not limited to, how the drug may be produced, its interactions with the inert components or vehicles that may hold it together, its best delivery form (taken by mouth, injected, inhaled, etc.), and even large-scale manufacturing.

Preclinical Testing

We are all aware of the lengths that the FDA goes to to protect our citizens. Preclinical testing provides the FDA with one of its primary tools to ensure safety and collect data vital to move the new drug successfully through the approval process.

Voluminous testing at the laboratory bench in cell culture or in animal models is conducted to determine a handful of candidates that later will be studied in clinical trials. Although many factors are considered, efficacy and safety rank at the top, and the data must be compelling and reproducible.

IND Application

The filing of an investigational new drug application (IND) with the FDA is an important milestone marking the inter-section of investigational chemical development with the regulatory apparatus. The IND includes the accrued data from the previous bench work and preclinical trials. More-over, the IND must describe an expanded plan for a clinical trial.

The FDA isn't the only governing body policing the prog-ress across the threshold between preclinical and clinical testing. The institutions at which trials will be performed have a powerful mechanism to ensure safety of the study participants, the institutional review board (IRB).

Essentially every AMC and research university has an IRB. This body is composed of researchers, clinicians, statis-ticians, and administrators who understand the processes of large-scale investigation involving human subjects. IRBs have experience in study design and the specific focus of develop-ing the appropriate informed consent required from potential study participants.

From this point, regular, detailed information exchange will take place between the sponsoring organization and the

FDA. If safety concerns arise, either the institution or the FDA can halt the trial. Trials of investigational drugs also have been truncated because the nascent therapy is so effective that it would be considered unethical to subject it to an even more lengthy regulatory process. Regardless of eventual outcome, the IND is one of the most critical stages in drug development.

Clinical Trials

The compounds have passed through multiple steps designed to weed out characteristics that could be considered harmful or render the molecule(s) ineffective. The ultimate laboratory is the human subject.

Not only are students of innovation familiar with the phases of clinical trials, even popular media often report promising new drugs transitioning from one phase to another. The phases of clinical trials have become almost common vernacular, as anxious and engaged observers who suffer from specific diseases closely follow the progress of promising compounds.

The three main phases demonstrate a logical progression, from testing in healthy volunteers to larger groups of patients afflicted with the target disease or disorder. In Phase 1, usually 50 to 100 healthy subjects receive the candidate drug. Roughly the same pharmacokinetic battery of testing described earlier (ADME/tox) is conducted. The response of the subjects (not considered patients) is monitored through clinical and laboratory examinations. Parameters like dosage ranges may be manipulated during this phase, while the drug is evaluated for safety and effectiveness.

In Phase 2 clinical trials, the candidate drug touches patients for the first time. Proven safe and effective in healthy volunteers, a set of patients with the disease or disorder receive the drug and are monitored for side effects ranging from allergies to drug interactions. The developers and principal investigators evaluate the clinical response to the drug: is it affecting the disease state in a predictable way?

Statisticians and clinicians work side by side during all phases, but especially in the transition between phases 2 and 3, to determine how many patients must receive the candidate drug to ensure statistical significance. The typical size of the study population in Phase 2 may be 100 to 500, but in Phase 3, the number is perhaps 10 times larger.

Phase 3 trials are both the lengthiest and most expensive. While a Phase 2 trial conceivably could be conducted at a single hospital or integrated healthcare system, Phase 3 requires a multicenter trial network carefully coordinated by the principal investigator.

Conducting large-scale clinical trials is a commercial activity of its own; in fact, it's big business. An estimated nearly 40,000 new drugs or devices are being tested in clinical trials at any given time. Rarely would this specific endeavor reside within an innovation and commercialization function like Cleveland Clinic Innovations. Clinical trials typically are orchestrated by industry experts who call upon veterans at leading AMCs or in private medical offices who engage frequently in such studies.

NDA

If all systems are go after the three sequential clinical trial phases, it's time to prepare the voluminous new drug application (NDA) for submission to the FDA. In addition to all of the data aggregated in the steps just outlined, descriptions of how the drug will be manufactured at scale and labeled for physician prescribers and the public is included in the NDA.

There is no single formula that leads to FDA approval or denial of a new drug. As the agency sifts through tens of thousands of pages of data detailing years of work and scrutiny of the new compound, the FDA is essentially weighing a risk/benefit ratio. No drug presents zero risk. It is the purview of the FDA to determine whether the associated risks outweigh the inherent benefits.

The FDA maintains extraordinary expertise in determining drug safety and efficacy. The FDA also enlists advisory committees composed of experts in particular fields, unassociated with the commercial development of the specific drug. Although the FDA often follows the recommendations of the advisory committees, it is not required to do so.

The drug can be approved, denied, or deemed approvable, which requires the sponsor to provide additional information.

Manufacture and Scaling

It is no mean task to move from research-scale compound preparation to commercial grade drug production. Even a slight variation in the composition of a drug is unacceptable for obvious reasons. Essentially every drug is distinct in its method of manufacture, so new or repurposed facilities are required. The FDA also has guidelines for good manufacturing practices (GMP) that must be met to engage in industrial-scale production of drugs. Constant testing for quality is conducted by both the commercial concerns and independent agencies. Action plans to stop production and even recall medicines must be in place.

Phase 4 Testing

Phase 4 clinical trials are conducted on patients who have been taking a specific new drug to detect its long-term effects.

These trials are conducted over extremely lengthy periods involving the monitoring of massive numbers of patients.

This episodic or continuous monitoring checks long-term safety and efficacy profiles and determines unique, subtle effects. The testing requires what statisticians call *power*, which allows calculation of the minimum sample size required to demonstrate an effect of a given magnitude. As power increases, the chance for false negative results decreases.

Drug discovery is arduous and expensive. For the patients in need, and those engaged in the odyssey to bring new compounds to market, the transit from the medicinal chemistry performed at the laboratory bench to the shelf of the pharmacy or hospital formulary can't be fast enough. However, public safety is the paramount concern. Among all the domains of contemporary innovation, the development of "molecules" (diagnostics and therapeutics) may require the most time, money and level of collaboration between the public, academic and private sectors.

Appendix

C

Sample Medical Innovation Maturity Survey (MiMS) Results

The intent of the MiMS is to define objectively an organization's cultural innovation maturity. Forty-two individuals completed the entire MiMS. While the number of respondents is fewer than anticipated, it is sufficiently significant to understand the organization's innovation status. The overall survey has a maximum score of 100. Figure C.1 shows SAMPLE's average score broken down by major job categories. In parentheses are the numbers of individuals completing the entire survey for that job category. The median score is 42.7. The mean score is 40.08. The lowest score is 11.24, one of 12 scores that was under 20 points (all from respondents who categorized themselves as physicians), and the highest score is 76.20 (C-suite individual). The disparity in scoring by job category is the highest ever seen in an organization completing the MiMS, indicating a significant divergence in opinion of SAMPLE's people,

FIGURE C.1 SAMPLE M*i*MS Results

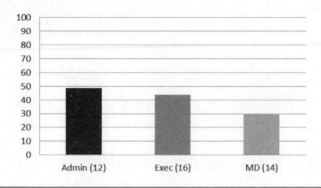

process, and philosophy associated with innovation and commercialization.

Overall, scores are low when compared to organizations with a fairly robust commercialization office. However, lower scores are expected and not unusual for organizations that don't have a functioning commercialization arm. The scores for each job group are fairly consistent with the answers given during the Graded Perspective Analysis (GPA) individual interviews. The scores of most organizations surveyed fall within a fairly tight range, but SAMPLE has a significant deviation in scoring range.

There is a clear difference in scoring between clinicians/physicians and the administration/executive level, as also seen in the GPA. Executive and administration leaders answered that the organization is far more mature in its commercialization and innovation structure and has a significantly stronger infrastructure in place. Executive and nonphysician administration M*i*MS scores are almost 60 percent higher than those of physicians. This is a clear and strong message that organizational support for innovation has not been effectively communicated to physician staff.

FIGURE C.2 SAMPLE M*i*MS Scores by Question

	Average Score	Total Possible Score
Q1	2.07	3
Q2	2.04	3
Q3	1.07	3
Q4	2.1	3
Q5	0.43	3
Q6A	1.7	3.75
Q6B	0.51	1.25
Q7	5.7	10
Q8	3.25	5
Q9A	1.45	2.5
Q9B	1.35	2.5
Q10	1.97	5
Q11	0.42	5
Q12	4.49	10
Q13	4.32	10
Q14	5.23	10
Q15	1.06	10
Q16	3.52	10

Unfortunately, a significant number of physicians asked to take the M*i*MS either didn't begin or didn't complete the survey. The lack of participation by key stakeholders provides a data point regarding how engaged they are in the innovation and commercialization function. Physicians scored the organization as having little, if any, infrastructure in place and little support for innovation and commercialization.

On the M*i*MS, executive leaders scored an average of 43.8 on a 100-point scale. Physician scores were significantly lower, averaging 35.66, while administration's average score was 36.44. For benchmark comparison, organizations with established commercialization functions typically score around 73. As indicated earlier, the 60 percent differential in scores between physicians and administrators should serve as a catalyst for evaluating how innovation opportunities, organizational capabilities, and effective innovative changes are communicated to staff.

Overall, the organization's score concludes that there is an organizational need to implement or adjust numerous functions in support of a comprehensive, sustainable commercialization program. Capabilities must also be communicated to staff in a manner that engages and supports them throughout the commercialization process.

The average MiMS scores by question and the total possible average scores per question are noted in Figure C.2. The two questions receiving the highest responses are Q1 and Q4. Q1 asked whether innovations are encouraged/accepted from one or more of constituent groups. As noted earlier, self-identified SAMPLE executives scored this question very highly (2.13), while physicians scored this question significantly lower (1.56). Q4, which asked about dedicated physical and virtual space for innovation, had the second highest score. Again, self-identified SAMPLE executives scored this question very highly (2.30). Physicians scored this question considerably lower (1.17), indicating a lack of awareness of space, resources, and support capabilities for innovation.

Conversely, Q5 and Q15 were the lowest. Q5 dealt with marketing infrastructure. Q15 asked what resources the institution directly invests or leverages for commercialization purposes. Both questions are tied to capabilities and infrastructure currently in place to support innovation and commercialization. Most respondents score the organization poorly regarding capabilities in place to support commercialization.

Historically, MiMS scores are lower at community-based health providers compared to academic medical centers. Because community-based systems typically lack significant research operations and funding for invention, ideas come from a much smaller portion of the staff population. Ideas are usually intermittent, opportunistic "lighting strikes," as opposed to by-products of strategic ideation around identified unmet market needs.

The MiMS looks at three distinct areas of innovation maturity within the organization:

- **People.** Provides an understanding of the individuals in place and their commercialization skill set, as well as the associated physician staff's desire and sophistication with regard to the commercialization process.

- **Process.** Policies, procedures, and infrastructure in place to support commercialization activities.

- **Philosophy.** Overall support for innovation across the organization. This includes the celebration of both successes and failures, the administration for inventors, and the handling of disruptive changes through new procedures and treatments that improve existing patient treatments.

People

MiMS questions relating to the human resource support and skill set of individuals in place across the enterprise for commercialization of innovations have the most widespread variability in answers. When asked whether innovation was accepted across various constituent levels in the organization (Q1), self-identified SAMPLE executives indicate that all constituents, including external innovators, are encouraged to bring ideas to the organization for development and implementation. Self-identified physicians and patient caregivers had a much more modest response, with nearly a third indicating that innovation is encouraged and accepted only by executives and physicians. This inconsistency in scoring between constituency levels is seen throughout the M*i*MS results.

When asked how connected the organization is with the marketplace (Q10), SAMPLE executives gave SAMPLE significantly higher scores than physicians. Most executive-level respondents indicated that SAMPLE is connected to the marketplace with semi-structured exchanges on innovation to fill its core needs. On the other hand, physicians answered that the organization either is disconnected or has more of a client/vendor commercialization relationship.

Overall, SAMPLE executives identified SAMPLE as having much more full-bodied innovation opportunities, internal and external relationships, and investment in the people component of innovation.

Process

The most aligned scores among all individuals, regardless of identified position within the organization, were related to questions about the processes in place for innovation and commercialization support. Most individuals answered that the organization does not have significant processes in place. Most responded that aligned and understood innovation and commercialization metrics are not disseminated or embraced by the organization (Q3). The majority of individuals answered that metrics employed for innovation across the institution are in place, but not disseminated or embraced.

When asked about dedicated space for innovation (Q4), executives generally answered that there is laboratory or incubator space for innovation. Nonexecutives typically said that there is no space or only borrowed space for innovation. This question has the least alignment based on the identified position of the respondent.

Overall, the second most consistent answer relates to the question on communication and marketing infrastructure supporting the innovation platform (Q5). Seventy-five percent of respondents indicated that there is a limited amount of internal communication and no external awareness. This answer is fairly common in an organization that doesn't have a dynamic innovation process in place.

Philosophy

The most consistent answer to the questions around philosophy (culture) involved the domains of innovation being cultivated in the organization (Q6). More than 90 percent of respondents indicated that the organization focuses solely on supporting innovation related to institutional process/know-how. These findings are consistent with what was communicated during the interview process and aligns with answers given about resources available for commercialization.

Innovation is often categorized as fast, frugal failure, with commercially viable opportunities quickly identified and acted upon. Successful innovative organizations celebrate innovation and believe that participation, recognition, and reward are critical for program success. Most physicians indicated that SAMPLE has a tolerant or permissive environment for innovation but lacks a celebrated culture (Q8). SAMPLE executives tended to answer that the organization supports innovation and has resources in place to support proof of concept without negative consequences resulting from a failed attempt.

Figure C.3 summarizes where SAMPLE falls on the innovation maturity bell curve. Overall, scores from the M*i*MS put SAMPLE just above the bottom tier. Without some modest innovation success in business processes, SAMPLE would most likely fall near or below the bottom tier. Recognize that

FIGURE C.3 SAMPLE M*i*MS Maturity on the Bell Curve

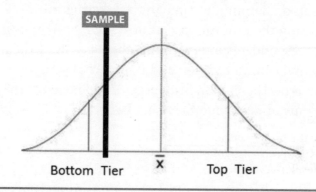

the focus of the M*i*MS and other components of the diagnostic looked at translating ideas and opportunities outside the organization.

Based on the M*i*MS survey, there is a clear disconnect in the understanding of capabilities, support, and innovation infrastructure response. High-level administration identifies the organization as being much more capable and encouraging of innovation than other groups across the organization. The capabilities that leadership believes it has in place have not cascaded throughout the organization and in particular have not been identified as a strong suit by physicians employed by the organization and those physicians working at a SAMPLE facility.

The lack of understanding around innovation maturity requires the organization to review its capabilities and determine more precisely what support is truly available. These capabilities must then be communicated across the enterprise, supported, and continually reintroduced to all constituents on a consistent basis.

Notes

Chapter 1

1 For the history of the founding of Cleveland Clinic, see John D. Clough, *To Act as a Unit: The Story of the Cleveland Clinic* (Cleveland: Cleveland Clinic Press, 2005).

2. Merritt Hawkins, *Review of Physician Recruiting Incentives: An Overview of the Salaries, Bonuses, and Other Incentives Customarily Used to Recruit Physicians* (2012), http://www .merritthawkins.com/uploadedFiles/MerrittHawkins/Pdf/ mha2012incentivesurveyPDF.pdf.

3. Data derived from Centers for Medicare & Medicaid Services Case Mix Indices, as reported on the American Hospital Directory website, www.ahd.com.

4. U.S. Government Accounting Office, "Technology Transfer, Administration of the Bayh-Dole Act by Research Universities," *Report to Congressional Committees*, May 7, 1978.

Chapter 2

1. Theodore Roosevelt, "Citizenship in a Republic" (address, l'Université Paris-Sorbonne, Paris, April 23, 1910), accessed March 30, 2015, http://www.theodore-roosevelt.com/ trsorbonnespeech.html.

2. Biotech Industry Organization, *The Economic Contributions of University/Nonprofit Inventions in the United States: 1996–2010* (2012), accessed March 26, 2015, https://www.bio.org/articles/ economic-contribution-universitynonprofit-inventions-united -states-1996-2010.

3. Association of University Technology Managers (AUTM), *U.S. Licensing Survey* (2013), accessed May 25, 2015, http://www .autm.net/FY_2013_Licensing_Activity_Survey/15156.htm.

Chapter 3

1. Vilfredo Pareto (1848–1923), an Italian economist, published *Cours d'économie politique* in 1896, describing that 80 percent of the land in his native country was held by 20 percent of the

population. His hypothesis came from noting that 20 percent of the pea pods in his garden produced 80 percent of the crop. "Pareto Principle," *Wikipedia*, last modified April 7, 2015, accessed April 8, 2015, http://en.wikipedia.org/wiki/Pareto _principle.
2. The Global Healthcare Innovations Alliance is discussed in detail in Chapter 6.
3. Jeff Dyer, Hal Gregersen, and Clayton M. Christensen, *The Innovator's DNA: Mastering the Five Skills of Disruptive Innovators* (Boston: Harvard Business Review Press, 2011).
4. Tom Kelley and Jonathan Littman, *The Ten Faces of Innovation: IDEO's Strategies for Defeating the Devil's Advocate and Driving Creativity Throughout Your Organization* (New York: Currency/ Doubleday, 2005).
5. Dyer et al., 11.
6. Henry Doss, "Five Ways Incentives Kill Innovation," *Forbes*, December 19, 2013.
7. Kristen Grabarz, "Want Tenure at Penn? Be Innovative," *The Daily Pennsylvanian*, November 12, 2014.
8. Kelley and Littman, 75–77.

Chapter 4

1. The Global Healthcare Innovations Alliance is discussed thoroughly in Chapter 6.
2. For additional information on Cleveland Clinic's institute structure, see Toby Cosgrove, *The Cleveland Clinic Way* (New York: McGraw-Hill, 2013), 38–44.

Chapter 5

1. Diana Furchtgott-Roth and Harold Furchtgott-Roth, *Employment Effects of the New Excise Tax on the Medical Device Industry* (Washington, D.C.: Advanced Medical Technology Association, July 2011), accessed September 9, 2015, http:// advamed.org/res.download/290.
2. Paul N. van de Water, *Excise Tax on Medical Devices Should Not Be Repealed* (Washington, D.C.: Center on Budget and Policy Priorities, February 23, 2015), accessed September 9, 2015, http://www.cbpp.org/sites/default/files/atoms/files/2-14 -12health.pdf.
3. *Estimated Revenue Effects of Division I of H.R. 4, the "Jobs for America Act"* (Washington, D.C.: Joint Committee on Taxation, Congress of the United States, September 17, 2014),

Publication JCX-105-14, accessed September 9, 2015, www.jct
.gov/publications.html?func=startdown&id=4672. The Joint
Commission's initial estimate in March 2010 overestimated the
revenue raised by the tax.

4. Frank Papay, "The Challenges Facing Medical Device
Companies," in *The Medical Innovation Playbook* (Cleveland:
Cleveland Clinic Innovations, 2013): 70–81.

5. James Manyika, Michael Chui, Brad Brown, Jacques Bughin,
Richard Dobbs, Charles Roxburgh, and Angela Hung Byers,
*Big Data: The Next Frontier for Innovation, Competition, and
Productivity* (San Francisco: McKinsey Global Institute, 2011).

6. http://data.worldbank.org/indicator/SH.XPD.PCAP.

7. Frank Lichtenberg, *Benefits and Costs of Newer Drugs: An
Update* (Cambridge, Massachusetts: National Bureau of
Economic Research, June 2002), Working Paper 8996, accessed
September 9, 2015, http://www.nber.org/papers/w8996.

8. Ibid.

9. Kevin M. Murphy and Robert H. Topel, "The Value of Health
and Longevity," *Journal of Political Economy* 114, no. 5 (2006):
871–904.

10. Ross DeVol, Armen Bedroussian, et al., *An Unhealthy America:
The Economic Burden of Chronic Disease—Charting a New
Course to Save Lives and Increase Productivity and Economic
Growth* (Santa Monica, California: The Milken Institute,
October 2007).

11. Isaac Ehrlich and Gary S. Becker, "Market Insurance, Self-
Insurance, and Self-Protection," *Journal of Political Economy*
80, no. 4 (July–August 1972): 623–648.

12. Darius Lakdawalla, Anup Malnani, and Julian Reif,
The Insurance Value of Medical Innovation (Cambridge,
Massachusetts: National Bureau of Economic Research, 2015),
Working Paper 21015, accessed September 9, 2015, http://www
.nber.org/papers/w21015.

Chapter 6

1. Peter Drucker, *Innovation and Entrepreneurship: Practice and
Principles* (New York: Harper and Row, 1985). Excerpted in
"The Discipline of Innovation," *Harvard Business Review* 80, no.
8 (August 2002): 95–100, 102, 148. Drucker's seven sources of
innovation are unexpected occurrences, incongruities, process
needs, industry and market changes, demographic changes,
changes in perception, and new knowledge.

2. In addition to Drucker, I owe homage to the Hungarian author Frigyes Karinthy, from whose 1929 short story came the "six degrees of separation" concept. Frigyes Karinthy, *Everything Is Different* (Hungary: 1929).
3. Chad T. Wilson, Elliott S. Fisher, H. Gilbert Welch, Andrea E. Siewers, F. Lee Lucas, "U.S. Trends in CABG Hospital Volume: The Effect of Adding Cardiac Surgery Programs," *Health Affairs* 26:1 (2007): 162–168.
4. "Our Values at Work," International Business Machines Corporation, accessed February 19, 2015, http://www.ibm.com/ibm/values/us/.
5. *Breast Cancer Facts & Figures 2013–2014* (Atlanta: American Cancer Society, 2014).
6. For further information, see http://www.medicalinnovationplaybook.com/.

Chapter 7

1. Donald Hebb was the first to suggest that the "efficiency" of a given neuron, in contributing to the firing of another, could increase as that cell is repeatedly involved in the activation of the second. Thus, the basic tenet of Hebbian learning in neural networks is that "units that fire together, wire together." Donald O. Hebb, *The Organization of Behavior* (New York: Wiley, 1949). Cited in Yuko Munakata and Jason Pfaffly, "Hebbian Learning and Development," *Developmental Science* 7:2 (2004): 141–48.
2. Jessica Leber, "Economist Proposes a $30-Billion Megafund for New Cancer Drugs: A Hedge Fund Manager Aims to Solve the Funding Problems Facing Early-Stage Biomedical Research," *MIT Technology Review*, November 19, 2012. See also Jose-Maria Fernandez, Roger M. Stein, and Andrew W. Lo, "Commercializing Biomedical Research Through Securitization Techniques," *Nature Biotechnology* 30 (September 30, 2012): 964–75.

Chapter 8

1. Frans Johansson, *The Medici Effect: Breakthrough Insights at the Intersection of Ideas, Concepts, and Cultures* (Boston: Harvard Business Review Press, 2004).
2. See Peter Relan, "90% of Incubators and Accelerators Will Fail and That's Just Fine for America and the World," *Tech Crunch* (blog), October 14, 2012, http://techcrunch.com/2012/10/14/90-of-incubators-and-accelerators-will-fail-and-why-thats-just

-fine-for-america-and-the-world/. See also Tim Devaney and Tom Stein, "Startup Accelerator Fail: Most Graduates Go Nowhere," *Readwrite* (blog), June 21, 2012, http://readwrite.com/2012/06/21/startup-accelerator-fail-most-graduates-go-nowhere and Eilene Zimmerman, "Assessing the Impact of Business Incubators," in *You're the Boss: The Art of Running a Small Business* (blog), *New York Times*, August 12, 2013, http://boss.blogs.nytimes.com/2013/08/12/assessing-the-impact-of-business-incubators/?_r=0.

3. Michael Porter, "Clusters and Competition: New Agendas for Companies, Governments, and Institutions," *Harvard Business School Working Paper*, No. 98-080, March 1998.

4. Joe Andre, Ziona Austrian, and Matthew Hrubey, *The Cleveland Health Tech Corridor: An Analysis of Economic Trends, 2000–2011* (Cleveland: Cleveland State University, Maxine Goodman Levin College of Urban Affairs, 2012).

5. Brie Zeltner, "Cleveland Clinic Worth $12.6 Billion to Ohio, Report Says," *Plain Dealer*, April 30, 2015.

Chapter 9

1. For further reading on the venture philanthropist class, see Matthew Bishop and Michael Green, *Philanthrocapitalism: How the Rich Can Save the World* (New York: Bloomsbury Press, 2008); Joel L. Fleishman, *The Foundation: A Great American Secret; How Private Wealth Is Changing the World* (New York: Public Affairs, 2007); and Holden Thorp and Buck Goldstein, *Engines of Innovation: The Entrepreneurial University in the Twenty-First Century* (Chapel Hill: University of North Carolina Press, 2010).

2. Jamie Merrill, "Number of Global Billionaires Has Doubled Since the Financial Crisis," *The Independent*, October 29, 2014, accessed online April 6, 2015, http://www.independent.co.uk/news/world/politics/number-of-global-billionaires-has-doubled-since-the-financial-crisis-9826345.html.

3. Bill Gates, "Who We Are," *Annual Letter 2009*, January 2009, accessed April 6, 2015, http://www.gatesfoundation.org/who-we-are/resources-and-media/annual-letters-list/annual-letter-2009.

4. Steven Lawrence and Reina Mukai, *Foundation Growth and Giving Estimates: Current Outlook* (New York: The Foundation Center, 2010).

5. Stated in homage to Marshall McLuhan's famous 1978 saying, "The medium is the message."

Chapter 10

1. In addition to Cleveland Clinic, the Global Cardiovascular Innovation Center collaborators include Case Western Reserve University, Ohio State University, University of Cincinnati, University Hospitals Health System, and University of Toledo.
2. Jose-Maria Fernandez, Roger M. Stein, and Andrew W. Lo, "Commercializing Biomedical Research Through Securitization Techniques," *Nature Biotechnology* 30 (September 30, 2012): 964–75.
3. "Where are they now?" excerpts, the Cleveland Clinic Innovations Top 10 Innovations from 2007–2015, can be found at http://innovations.clevelandclinic.org/Summit-(1)/Top-10 -Innovations.aspx#.VTbQ7iFVhBc.

Index

About the Author

Thomas J. Graham, MD, is the Chief Innovation Officer of Cleveland Clinic. He leads the technology commercialization and corporate venturing arm of the Ohio-based global healthcare system, where he holds the Justice Family Chair in Medical Innovations. He is also the Vice-Chairman of the Department of Orthopaedic Surgery.

Dr. Graham has extensive clinical expertise in surgery of the hand, wrist, and elbow, with special concentration on complicated reconstruction after trauma, complex elbow disorders, and congenital hand surgery. His practice is recognized worldwide as the premier destination for care of the wrist and hand of the professional athlete and entertainer.

His orthopaedic surgery career began at Cleveland Clinic in 1993, where he later became Chief of the Hand and Upper Extremity Division. In 2000, Dr. Graham was appointed Director of the Congressionally designated Curtis National Hand Center, the world's largest practice in the specialty, located in Baltimore, Maryland. While there, he was as an associate professor of both orthopaedic and plastic surgery at Johns Hopkins. He also served as Director of MedStar SportsHealth, the sports operations division of the largest healthcare system in the mid-Atlantic. In 2006, he launched the Arnold Palmer Sports Health Center to honor his longtime friend and patient.

In 2010, Dr. Graham, a serial entrepreneur and prolific inventor with nearly 50 issued and pending patents, returned to Cleveland Clinic and was named the inaugural Chief Innovation Officer.

Dr. Graham has served as the hand surgery consultant or team physician for professional sports organizations in the four major North American leagues, as well as the PGA and LPGA Tours. He has published over 100 scholarly articles and has edited several books. He was featured on ABC's *Nightline* for his role in the treatment of 9/11 survivors. His involvement with these heroes was also chronicled in an exhibit at the Smithsonian Institution. He has also been featured on the Golf Channel, ESPN, and *The Daily Show with Jon Stewart*, and many other media outlets.

A graduate of Williams College, he received his MD from the University of Cincinnati College of Medicine. He completed his residency training in orthopaedic surgery at the University of Michigan and a fellowship in hand and upper extremity surgery at the famed Indiana Hand Center. He was a visiting surgeon at the Mayo Clinic, studying surgery of the elbow. He completed the executive management program in healthcare administration jointly sponsored by Cleveland Clinic and the Weatherhead School of Management at Case Western Reserve University.

Dr. Graham is involved in multiple civic initiatives and organizations, especially those that advance innovation, community health, and economic development. An accomplished golfer and outdoorsman, he is married to his childhood sweetheart, CeCe, with whom he has two adult daughters, Margaret and Elizabeth.